Roads of Reformation

Proven Models & Methods

Roads of Reformation
Proven Models & Methods

CI Publishing
PO Box 9000
Santa Rosa Beach, Florida 32459
800-388-5308
www.christianinternational.com

ISBN: 978-0-939868-80-3
Printed in the United States of America

Roads of Reformation: Proven Models & Methods was compiled
by Catherine M Lovett, PhD, ABD. Catherine has been
instrumental in the development of hundreds of resources made
available through Christian International Marketplace Resources.
She has served in the area of marketplace ministry, marketing, and
resource development for the last three decades and has an
understanding of the importance of the 7 Mountain mandate. A
seasoned speaker and instructor, Catherine brings revelation of the
7 Mountain mandate to the Body of Christ.

CONTENTS

INTRODUCTION

EKKLESIA

by Larry Bizette

According to Ephesians 4:11-12, pulpit ministers have the responsibility to teach saints to do the work of the ministry. As ministers in the marketplace, our job is to model Jesus Christ in the workplace. Statistically, approximately 98 percent of the people in church congregations spend most of their waking hours actively working. Therefore, both sets of "ministers" are responsible to be "Kingdom" focused, bringing the Kingdom of God into the (world) workplace.

We (the Church) have been deceived into thinking the Kingdom of God will manifest in the future, that our perspective of "church" is reduced to a physical building, and the marketplace is a place where people are forced to work to survive. Unfortunately, except for salvation, many Christians do not understand who they are in Christ, or their divine purpose and calling in God's Kingdom. Many Christians feel inadequate because they are business people and not "ministers." But scripture is clear that all believers are called to be kings and priests (Revelation 5:10), and most believers fulfill His kingly order within the marketplace.

Jesus' ministry on earth caused a major paradigm shift in people's understanding of God's Kingdom. Jesus referred to God's Kingdom as present (Matthew 12:28), eminent (Mark 9:1), and in the future (Matthew 26-29, Mark 14:25). His focus was not on the temple but on taking the message of the Kingdom to the marketplace where people were. Joseph, Daniel, Esther, David, Paul, Barnabus, and Stephen, all biblical examples of marketplace ministers, understood that their focus must be about God's Kingdom being alive and thriving within the workplace. If all believers would go to work fully convinced that they are on assignment and worshipping God through their labor, then they would feel empowered to make a difference thus transforming their communities, cities, and nations.

The word church in Matthew 16:18 stems from the Greek word ekklesia, meaning to summon forth. Historically the term referred to the assembling of citizens of an ancient Greek state. The same word in Ecclesiastical terms refers to the church or congregation.

Therefore, historically, "the church" or His Saints are ones called to assemble as citizens to make policy decisions for the city. We, His church, are called to affect the economic, judicial, political, and educational policies of society. This is the calling and purpose of the local church. Today, more than ever before, we are called to make a difference, "and upon this rock [He] will build [His] church; and the gates of hell shall not prevail against it" (KJV).

Across the Body of Christ, Saints are receiving the revelation that not all of us are called to full-time pulpit ministry, but all Christians are full-time ministers. Each of us has the power and the authority to transform our spheres of influence. We must shift from just simply knowing to actually understanding the power and authority we have to walk in His anointing. In order to accomplish this, we must be involved with the city council, the school board, and the state legislature. We must teach marketplace ministers how to work in unity as a valuable resource in each community. The only way that we can transform a city is by the church, the marketplace, and the local civil government working together in unity.

Revelation 11:15 says, "The kingdoms of this world have become the kingdoms of our Lord and of His Christ, and He shall reign forever and ever!" We, the Saints, must arise to take our place and fulfill our part in seeing "the kingdoms of this world become the kingdoms of our Lord and of His Christ."

 **Larry Bizette** worked in the banking industry for 20 years as Senior Vice President and Branch Administrator. Larry was instrumental in establishing a Commercial and Retail Lending Program for branch officers, resulting in a portfolio growing from three million to twenty million dollars in a two year period with a write-off ratio of less than one percent. In the same period, he developed and implemented an Officer Call Program to attract new business in a declining economy, affecting a 49% deposit growth. He also worked closely with senior management and employees during this time to realize a dramatic reduction in employee turnover − from 62% to 12%!

Larry and his wife Brenda, Founders of Antioch Family Church in Baton Rouge, LA, were ordained by Dr. Bill Hamon in June 1990. Established in July of 1990 Antioch is a network church under the Christian International Apostolic Network where Larry also serves as the Apostle of Marketplace and Government. Larry and Brenda serve on the Board of Governors for Bill and Evelyn Hamon.

In 2006, Larry established the Global Marketplace Alliance, an organization focused on impacting and transforming cities and nations for the Kingdom of God. Larry earned a B.S. in Business from Louisiana State University and degrees from the School of Banking of the South and the University of Oklahoma Commercial Lending School. Larry also earned a Masters of Biblical Studies from the Christian International School of Theology

1

THE KINGDOM OF GOD

by Dr. Tim Hamon

The message of the Kingdom of God is not new. Jesus preached the Kingdom while he was on earth. What is new (or restored) for our time is the revelation that the Kingdom must be manifest in our culture and society, not just in our churches.

7 MOUNTAINS

The picture we use to represent culture is commonly referred to as the "7 Mountains," where each of the 7 Mountains represents a major cultural influence. Typically, the 7 Mountains are identified as religion, government, business, family, media, arts/entertainment, and education.

The idea of describing our culture in these seven areas was first proposed over 30 years ago. The following is an account by Os Hillman of the first known instance:

In 1975, Bill Bright, founder of Campus Crusade, and Loren Cunningham, founder of Youth With a Mission, had lunch together in Colorado. God simultaneously gave each of them a message to give to the other. About a month later the Lord showed Francis Schaeffer the same thing.

> *Therefore, we can be missionaries... if you're a lawyer... if you're in Hollywood... if you're working as a doctor.*

In November of 2007 I (Os Hillman) had the privilege of interviewing Loren Cunningham, founder of Youth With a Mission. Following is an excerpt of that interview as he describes the meeting with Bill Bright that day.

"As we came in and greeted each other, (we were friends for quite a while), I was reaching for my yellow paper that I had written on the day before. And he said, 'Loren, I want to show you what God has shown me!' And it was virtually the same list that God had given me the day before. Three weeks later, my wife Darlene had seen Dr. Francis Schaeffer on TV and he had the same list! And so I realized that this was for the Body of Christ.

I gave it for the first time in Hamburg, Germany at the big cathedral there to a group of hundreds of young people that had gathered at that time. And I said, 'These are the areas that you can go into as missionaries. Here they are: First, it's the institution set up by God first, the family. After the family was church, or the people of God. The third was the area of school, or education. The fourth was media, public communication, in all forms, printed and electronic. The fifth was what I call celebration, the arts, entertainment, and sports, where you celebrate within a culture. The sixth would be the whole area of the economy, which starts with innovations in science and technology, productivity, sales, and service. The whole area, we often call it business, but we leave out sometimes the scientific part, which actually raises the wealth of the world. Anything new, like making sand into chips for a microchip, that increases wealth in the world. And then of course prediction sales and service helps to spread the wealth. And so the last was the area of government. Now government, the Bible shows in Isaiah 33 verse 22 that there are three branches of government, so it's all of the three branches: judicial, legislative, and executive. And then there are subgroups under all of those seven groups. And there are literally thousands upon thousands of sub-groups. But those seven can be considered like Caleb: 'Give me this mountain,' and they can be a 'mountain' to achieve for God. Or they can be a classroom that you're going to disciple a nation in. Because Jesus said, 'Go and disciple all nations.' And it also can affect us because in those areas we can be changed, transformed by the Holy Spirit to be effective missionaries into the area that God has called us into, and we will see it as not just a

3

job to get money to stay alive, but 'as the Father sent Me, so send I you,' Jesus said.

Therefore, we can be missionaries, where the word 'missionary' means 'one sent' and one sent of Jesus, if you're a lawyer in a legal office, you are sent of God. You're sent to be his missionary, or if you're in Hollywood, or you're working as a dentist, or you're working as a doctor, everything you can do for the glory of God. You may be in the area of foodservices. The Bible says in Zach 14:20 that even the cooking pots will be called 'holy' to the Lord. That's foodservices, or transportation. Everything from a bus driver to an airplane pilot or to a car dealer or whatever it is, it says even the veils of horses will be called holy to the Lord.

So we make whatever we do, if we do it as unto the Lord, a sanctified, or a holy work, it is Holy unto the Lord. It's not just the pulpit on Sunday, that's one of the spheres. It's also all the other spheres together, and that's how we achieve advancing the kingdom of God."

Loren proceeded to explain how they began to equip young people, with these 7 spheres in mind, through the schools they established all over the world.

The seven areas of culture are sometimes called institutions, spheres, or influence centers, but the most powerful image is the mountains. Even in the original discussion in 1975, the call to action was taken from Joshua 14:12, which says "give me this mountain." While the teaching excites us, we must ask first a most important question: Can we support this in scripture?

4

MOUNTAINS IN SCRIPTURE

Mountains are very important in scripture, literally and figuratively. A simple search shows over 450 biblical verses with mountains in them. Nearly every book of the Old Testament has at least one mountain verse, as do nine books of the New Testament. Of course, many of the references are simple geography: Mount Ararat (where Noah's Ark came to rest), Mount Sinai (where the Ten Commandments were inscribed), Mount of Olives (where Jesus prayed), and Mount Zion (where the Jerusalem was built).

> *The mountains in this scripture seem to represent influence or dominion. So... God's influence will be dominant over other influences.*

Although there are many literal geographical references to mountains, we should note that less than half of the mountain scriptures in the Old Testament are found in the narrative books of Genesis through II Chronicles. Actually, most of the mountain references in the Old Testament are in the wisdom books and the books of the major and minor prophets. So we can quickly say that the mountains in scriptures are not limited to simple geographic descriptions. Mountains obviously can have significant spiritual and symbolic meaning. While there are many interesting mountain scriptures in the prophetic books, the one that speaks the most to me about the 7 Mountains concept is found in the book of Isaiah.

THE MOUNTAIN OF THE LORD'S HOUSE

Now it shall come to pass in the latter days That the mountain of the LORD'S house Shall be established on the top of the mountains, And shall be exalted above the hills; And all nations shall flow to it. Many people shall come and say, "Come, and let us go up to the mountain of the Lord, To the house of the God of Jacob; He will teach us His ways, And we shall walk in His paths." For out of Zion shall go forth the law, And the word of the Lord from Jerusalem. (Isaiah 2:2-3 NKJV)

Verse two describes a spiritual mountain as "the mountain of the Lord's house," and this mountain of the Lord's house or temple "shall be established on top of the mountains." The mountains in this scripture seem to represent influence or dominion. So we could interpret this to mean that, in the last days, God's influence will be dominant over other influences.

The next phrase is "nations shall flow to it." The Hebrew word for nation is יּ, *gôy* . This word usually refers to a people group, which may or may not have a geopolitical identity but they do have a cultural identity, that is: origin, language, norms and governance. This is very similar to the Greek word that is usually translated nations ἔθνος *ethnos*. Both of these words can mean a nation like Mexico, but they can also mean a people group like a tribe or ethnic group. Or in our discussion, the "nation" could be the people group of government or the people group of education or religion, family, media, arts/entertainment, or business.

Verse three tells that "Many people shall come and say, 'Come, and let us go up to the mountain of the Lord, To the house

6

of the God of Jacob.'" When the people arrive at God's temple on His mountain, then "He will teach us His ways, And we shall walk in His paths." Then we will hear the voice of God: "For out of Zion shall go forth the law," the Hebrew word for law is torah, a precept or statute.[1] Torah signifies primarily direction, teaching, and instruction.[2] Torah might be considered the functional equivalent of the Greek word logos. Verse 3b says "and the word of the LORD from Jerusalem." The word for "word" is dabar, a word by implication spoken.[3] Dabar means to speak, say.[4] Dabar might be considered the functional equivalent of the Greek word rhema.

It seems like a weak offer on Satan's part to tempt Jesus with something He already knows is His.

Isaiah clearly uses the mountain as a picture of influence in the lives of people, and not just individuals but also people groups – nations. The mountain of Lord's house should be above or more influential than all the other mountains of influence so that the nations will come to receive the teaching of God. As you progress through the rest of Isaiah chapter two, you hear references to the influences that the mountain of the Lord's house will have over culture, government, morality, economics, and more.

---

[1] Strong's Talking Greek & Hebrew Dictionary
[2] Vine's Expository Dictionary of Old Testament and New Testament Words
[3] Strong's Talking Greek & Hebrew Dictionary
[4] Vine's Expository Dictionary of Old Testament and New Testament Words

MOUNTAINS – NATIONS - KINGDOMS

In Matthew chapter four, the New Testament has a similar picture to chapter two of Isaiah. This passage of scripture describes the devil's temptations of Jesus in the wilderness. Jesus has just been baptized by John and is immediately led by the Spirit into the wilderness to fast 40 days. At the end of the fast, Satan comes with three temptations. The first temptation is about Jesus' personal needs – turn stones to bread. The second temptation is about Jesus' relationship with the Father – protection from falling. But the third temptation is about the kingdoms of the world:

> *Again, the devil took Him up on an exceedingly high mountain, and showed Him all the kingdoms of the world and their glory. And he said to Him, "All these things I will give You if You will fall down and worship me." Then Jesus said to him, "Away with you, Satan! For it is written, 'You shall worship the Lord your God, and Him only you shall serve.'" (Matthew 4:8-10)*

First we notice that Satan takes Jesus up on a mountain. On this mountain, they can see all the kingdoms of the world. Of course, there is no literal mountain where you can see the whole world, so this is a spiritual place much like the mountain described in Isaiah 2 where all the nations are represented. On this mountain that is over the kingdoms of earth, the devil offers the kingdoms to Jesus. Jesus does not dispute that Satan has the power to make such an offer, but Jesus' response rather focuses on refusing the condition that He worship Satan. Not only does Jesus refuse Satan, but He also dismisses him as if there is no other temptation that could succeed once this temptation of the kingdoms has failed.

Frankly, the third temptation always puzzled me. The first two seem more obvious, that is, challenging Jesus' relationship with the Father regarding health (turning stones into bread) and then safety (preventing harm from a fall). The third temptation regards prosperity (Jesus' ownership of or authority over the earth and the kingdoms). It seems like a weak offer on Satan's part to tempt Jesus with something He already knows is His. Then I realized that the real temptation is in the way Jesus takes authority. Satan is offering a short cut to Jesus' inheritance that avoids the cross. We know that this is a powerful temptation for Jesus, since He confronts it again at Gethsemane: "He went a little farther and fell on His face, and prayed, saying, "O My Father, if it is possible, let this cup pass from Me; nevertheless, not as I will, but as You will." (Matthew 26:39)

Once Jesus successfully meets Satan's challenge, then He is ministered to by the angels and returns to Galilee where 'From that time Jesus began to preach and to say, "Repent, for the kingdom of heaven is at hand"' (Matthew 4:17). Apparently, when Jesus passed the kingdom test, that is when He began to preach the kingdom message.

7 MOUNTAINS CONTROLLED FOR GOOD OR EVIL

In Revelation chapter 17 we see the 7 Mountain image again. In this chapter, the seventh angel describes a "great harlot" sitting on seven mountains and many waters. Verse 9 explains the image: "Here *is* the mind which has wisdom: The seven heads are seven mountains on which the woman sits." Verse 15 continues, "The waters which you saw, where the harlot sits, are peoples, multitudes, nations, and tongues." This imagery looks very much like that of Isaiah 2 except the great harlot is trying to take the place of the Lord's house over the mountains to influence the peoples. It's clear that the great harlot represents Rome, known as the city built on seven hills. Verse 18 says, "And the woman whom you saw is that great city which reigns over the kings of the earth," but we can say Rome represents the seat of secular culture and influence in the nations.

The enemy wants to control the mountains (or kingdoms) of influence. We must be just like Jesus and refuse to give Satan the control. Rather, we will follow Jesus' command in Matthew 24:14: "And this gospel of the kingdom will be preached in all the world as a witness to all the nations, and then the end will come" so that we can fulfill Revelation 11:15: "The kingdoms of this world have become *the kingdoms* of our Lord and of His Christ, and He shall reign forever and ever!"

Dr. Tim Hamon is an apostolic-prophetic teacher whose life messages include leadership, reformation, and hearing the voice of God. Tim serves as the Chief Executive Officer of Christian International Ministries Network and is President of the Christian International School of Theology. He earned his Ph.D. in Organizational Leadership at Regent University in Virginia Beach, VA. Tim Hamon's first career included a decade in business and technology. He has been an ordained minister since 1988. With this background, he brings a full range of business, education, and ministry experience to his teaching. He travels to teach at various schools, conferences, and churches throughout the United States and internationally, including England, Italy, South Korea, Taiwan, Philippines, Bahamas, Scotland, and Israel. Tim and his wife Karen reside in Santa Rosa Beach, Florida. They have four children and four grandchildren.

2

RECLAIMING CULTURE: ONE COMMUNITY AT A TIME

by Os Hillman

And many of the Samaritans of that city believed in Him because of the word of the woman who testified..." (John 4:39).

C an a city or community be impacted for Christ? Can it be transformed? The answer to that lies with the level of maturity of that community's Christians, which is measured in love, unity, and prayer.

Jesus spent three years with His disciples, yet after three years, they thought the way to deal with different or adversarial people was to call down fire from heaven.

But they did not receive Him, because His face was set for the journey to Jerusalem. And when His disciples James and John saw this, they said, "Lord, do You want us to command fire to come down from heaven and consume them, just as Elijah did?" But He turned and rebuked them, and said, "You do not know what manner of spirit you are of. For the Son of Man did not come to destroy men's lives but to save them." And they went to another village (Luke 9:51-56).

The disciples modeled what the church does today. We condemn people who are different or hold different views, or we condemn them for acting like people who do not know God. The church has often tried to change culture by controlling it instead of loving it. Instead, Jesus calls us to love people and build bridges into their lives. Yes, that even means, gays, adulterers, and even liberals - yes, anyone different from ourselves.

> The church has often tried to change culture by controlling it instead of loving it.

Jesus loves them too, even in their sin. That is hard for us to model in the body of Christ. We all struggle to love those very different from ourselves.

In 2011 we had a conference at Harvard, and the speakers were protested on campus by radical gays. Instead of reacting to them, God made a way for me and another leader to meet with them. First, we listened to what they had to say. Afterwards, they let us share with them why their assessment of us was incorrect. Lastly, we upheld the relationship even though we had differing views. They left the meeting with a 180 degree different viewpoint than when they walked into it. Did they get saved? No. Did they have a different view of us than before they met us? Yes. Was there a bridge built? Yes. God can water that kind of relationship building, and He has actually done so since then.

"I CATCH THEM; THE LORD CLEANS THEM."

Larry Poland, President of MasterMedia, said at one of our conferences, "I catch them; the Lord cleans them." He serves executives in Hollywood and New York. He said, "You know, it is amazing how scripts change once there is a heart change." We are not the Holy Spirit in people's lives. Our role is to love and share. That's it. Then love some more.

JESUS AND THE SAMARITAN WOMAN

Let's discover how Jesus did it. Jesus interaction with the Samaritan woman set an example:

> *Then the woman of Samaria said to Him, "How is it that You, being a Jew, ask a drink from me, a Samaritan woman?" For Jews have no dealings with Samaritans. Jesus answered and said to her, "If you knew the gift of God, and who it is who says to you, 'Give Me a drink,' you would have asked Him, and He would have given you living water." The woman said to Him, "Sir, You have nothing to draw with, and the well is deep. Where then do You get that living water? Are You greater than our father Jacob, who gave us the well, and drank from it himself, as well as his sons and his livestock?" Jesus answered and said to her, "Whoever drinks of this water will thirst again, but whoever drinks of the water that I shall give him will never thirst. But the water that I shall give him will become in him a fountain of water springing up into everlasting life."*

15

The woman said to Him, "Sir, give me this water, that I may not thirst, nor come here to draw." Jesus said to her, "Go, call your husband, and come here." The woman answered and said, "I have no husband." Jesus said to her, "You have well said, 'I have no husband,' for you have had five husbands, and the one whom you now have is not your husband; in that you spoke truly." The woman said to Him, "Sir, I perceive that You are a prophet. Our fathers worshiped on this mountain, and you Jews say that in Jerusalem is the place where one ought to worship." Jesus said to her, "Woman, believe Me, the hour is coming when you will neither on this mountain, nor in Jerusalem, worship the Father. You worship what you do not know; we know what we worship, for salvation is of the Jews. But the hour is coming, and now is, when the true worshipers will worship the Father in spirit and truth; for the Father is seeking such to worship Him. God is Spirit, and those who worship Him must worship in spirit and truth." The woman said to Him, "I know that Messiah is coming" (who is called Christ). "When He comes, He will tell us all things." Jesus said to her, "I who speak to you am He." And at this point His disciples came, and they marveled that He talked with a woman; yet no one said, "What do You seek?" or, "Why are You talking with her?" The woman then left her waterpot, went her way into the city, and said to the men, "Come, see a Man who told me all things that I ever did. Could this be the Christ?" Then they went out of the city and came to Him (John 4:9-30, NKJV).

And many of the Samaritans of that city believed in Him because of the word of the woman who testified, "He told me all that I ever did." So when the Samaritans had come to Him, they urged Him to stay with them; and He stayed there two days. And many more believed because of His own word. Then they said to the woman, "Now we believe, not because of what you said, for we ourselves have heard Him and we know that this is indeed the Christ, the Savior of the world" (John 4:39-42).

Here is what Jesus did:
1. He listened and engaged in conversation.
2. He spoke into her life.
3. He gave her information and spoke prophetically.
4. He did not give her laws.
5. He did not condemn her.

Here is the result:
1. Her life was impacted by his speaking into her life.
2. She shared her experience with others.
3. The citizens of the city invited Jesus to stay for two days.
4. **Many believed in Jesus!**

That is your formula for community impact.

A GRASSROOTS MOVEMENT

Church leaders, business leaders, and intercessors are joining together in a collective effort to impact their city and community for Christ in Santa Rosa, California. It's an effort they call *Together in Christ.* Their simple strategy of *praying* together, *caring*, expressed by solving problems in the community that government simply cannot afford to address, and then *sharing* the love of Christ in their community is proving to be both effective

17

and sustainable. This has been going on for over eighteen years, but it wasn't until the marketplace got involved that leaders began to see real breakthrough in what they were doing. Today, this initiative has more than 60 churches involved, many of whom also partner with men and women in the marketplace for the purpose of impacting their city. Thousands of residents are being touched directly. The least and the last, the hurting and the hopeless, the isolated and the insulated are all seeing the gospel in action and are responding. The city's crime rates are improving while the regional, state, and national trends are heading the opposite direction. Recently, the city of Santa Rosa was recognized nationally as an "All American City." Now, city leaders are looking to *Together in Christ* as a partner in solving problems and seizing opportunities in the city. Deuteronomy 28:13 says that we are to become the head, not the tail. This can only happen when the collective local church serves the community in humility and through the love of Christ.

> *Their strategy of caring, expressed by solving problems in the community that government simply cannot afford to address, is proving effective and sustainable.*

A grassroots movement is taking place across the United States right now. It involves the formation of community-based Christian coalitions made up of local churches, workplace leaders, and intercessors desiring change in their communities. For the last ten years, I have seen this take place nationally and internationally. When God wants something started, He puts it into the heart of His people, and others begin to have similar initiatives, which all have a common thread to them.

In March of 2005, I was speaking in a conference in Red Deer, Canada. There were about 1,000 people in the audience when Cindy Jacobs made her way to the podium. Cindy is known for her prophetic ministry to nations and individuals. This was the second time Cindy has spoken over me, but never in a public setting like this. In that statement she said God was going to give me a model for city transformation that would be replicated around the world, but it would first begin in my own hometown. It would be several years after that when I would discover what that model was. Today I see that model being used in no less than 30 cities across the United States and also in other nations. If we are going to reclaim culture, I believe we must have local community transformation movements. It will mean that the seven cultural mountains will be affected on a localized level through these coalitions.

CITY TRANSFORMATION "TRINITY"

I believe there is a community transformation "trinity" of relationships that is key to community transformation. Three groups of people are vital to bringing change to the spiritual climate in a city or community: (1) intercessors, who are called to intercede for the city; (2) pastors and nuclear (or core) church leaders who have a vision for their cities; and (3) workplace leaders who want to use their marketplace influence for change within their communities. These men and women are called to impact their cities through their spheres of influence in the seven specific cultural mountains.

In 2003, the Lord impressed upon me that I was to start bringing Atlanta workplace leaders and ministries together for a vision of transforming the city. We partnered with the Billy Graham Evangelistic Association in April 2004 to host a workplace conference for the city. However, that meeting did not spark any ongoing initiatives.

Events are not what change a city... but they are a catalyst to get leaders working together.

I continued to meet with the workplace ministries, but nothing seemed to be happening. I kept trying to find intercessors in the city, but I was unsuccessful. Finally, I got to know Alistair Petrie when I had him speak at our international conference in October 2004. Alistair is an authority and researcher on city transformation. When I shared my frustration with him, he said, "Oh, you need to meet Jacquie Tyre. She is one of your key city intercessors." I met with Jacquie, and things immediately began to happen. I began connecting with some of the city church leaders.

A short time later, in February 2005, Graham Power, founder of Transformation Africa and the Global Day of Prayer, came through town. I was asked to host a meeting for Graham to share the vision of the Global Day of Prayer. Up to this point, the city had not made any decisions about joining this initiative, but that day about 100 leaders in the city came to hear Graham and, by the end of the meeting, made a commitment to hold an Atlanta Global Day of Prayer. Things started moving fast. Within 30 days, $225,000 was raised, a 20,000-seat venue was reserved, and the city began coming together. However, we have learned that events are not what change a city, but rather the catalyst to get leaders working together toward a common goal in the city.

I believe all this happened because these three groups of people came together in a unified effort to impact our city - intercessors, apostolic nuclear church leaders, and workplace leaders.

God is using workplace leaders to be the catalyst to bring the three core groups of people together more and more. Perhaps this is because workplace leaders don't have turf issues to wrestle with like local church leaders. I also discovered that not every local church pastor has a heart for their city. If a pastor has the gift and office of pastor, he often is more consumed with the needs of his local congregation. Only when the pastor has a more "apostolic" view of his community and exhibits a desire to impact the community at large is he willing to be involved in such an effort.

WHAT IS REQUIRED FOR CITY AND COMMUNITY TRANSFORMATION?

There are four key ingredients required among Christian leaders to see their city transformed. These include prayer, humility, unity and knowledge of God's ways. Let's discuss each of these.

Prayer

In every city in which transformation has taken place, believers have come together to pray for their city. Prayer changes the spiritual climate of a city. Some of the main areas of influence that our prayers must focus on include churches and businesses; the legal, political, educational, and medical fields; and the media/entertainment industry. "If my people, who are called by my name, will humble themselves and pray and seek my face and turn from their wicked ways, then will I hear from heaven and will forgive their sin and will heal their land" (2 Chronicles 7:14). Workplace leaders must be strategically aligned with intercessors to impact their city.

> *Those of us in the workplace are often zealous for God, but we can move in presumption instead of in faith that is rooted in knowledge.*

The late Swedish prayer leader, Kjell Sjoberg, who often read about his city transformation exploits in the next day's newspaper after their evening prayer initiatives, explained that we have to go through gates in order to get into a particular place:

> The gates are the key persons, the decision-makers, they are groups such as changers of commerce, political groups, orders, clubs, and large businesses. They are not our enemies. But we believe also that there are demonic principalities ruling over towns and places. They are to make use of key persons in a town, and these in turn become the closed gates of the town that hinder the representatives of the Kingdom of God from coming in and gaining influence for God's kingdom. In the gates of hell, councils are held to enable the principalities and the powers to gain control of the power bases built up in places and centers of population, and so maintain their

control in the world. The object of the power bases is to be able to resist invasion by the kingdom of heaven initiatives by Jesus Christ and continued by the church and by the hosts of angels supporting it. Our role is to be the invasion force that goes into the attack against the stronghold of hell. 'The Lord Almighty...will be a spirit of justice to him who sits in judgment, a source of strength to those who turn back the battle at the gate.' [5]

Humility

God uses men and women who recognize that they need each other and do not seek glory for their work. "He guides the humble in what is right and teaches them his way." [6] The workplace leaders whom God is using today care little about being in the limelight. The same is true of the shepherds of local churches in a community. When shepherds pastor their community, the turf wars begin to evaporate. Both leaders have a Kingdom perspective that avoids bringing attention to themselves or any one group in order to impact the city for Jesus Christ.

Unity

Jesus said, "May they be brought to complete unity to let the world know that you sent me and have loved them even as you have loved me." [7] God calls each of us individually and corporately to represent Christ to the world, but our independence, pride, and egos often prevent us from becoming unified in the purposes of Christ. We are scattered in our church affiliations and in our city transformation efforts. Unity is built when we roll up our sleeves

---

[5] Is 28:5-6
[6] Ps. 25:9
[7] John 17:23

23

and determine to work together - pastors, priests, and people from every walk of life. The marketplace and the Church must come together to bless the city with practical initiatives that benefit the city.

Knowledge of God's Ways

Those of us in the workplace are often zealous for God, but we can move in presumption instead of in a faith that is rooted in knowledge of God's ways. Such was the case of David, who wanted to bring the Ark of the Covenant into the city of Jerusalem. He was zealous for God and celebrated as he brought the Ark into the city. However, the ark was being carried into the city on a cart instead of by priests on poles, as God required. When a man named Uzzah reached out to catch the Ark when the oxen stumbled, he was immediately struck dead by God. "When they came to the threshing floor of Nacon, Uzzah reached out and took hold of the ark of God, because the oxen stumbled. The Lord's anger burned against Uzzah because of his irreverent act; therefore God struck him down and he died there beside the ark of God."[8] David was devastated.

We must connect with our priests and pastors to jointly work on bringing the presence of God into our cities. Otherwise, we will fail like David and be guilty of presumption. "For I can testify about them that they are zealous for God, but their zeal is not based on knowledge" (Romans 10:2).

Blessing the City

The final piece of the puzzle that has been missing in city transformation efforts is the intentional efforts to bless the city. Eric Swanson and Rick Rusaw have written a book titled, *The*

---

[8] 2 Sam 6:6-7

24

Externally Focused Church. This book cites a trend taking place across the nation in which churches are intentionally impacting social problems in the city. Eric was a speaker at our 2008 Reclaim 7 Mountains International Conference. He shared his thoughts on city transformation:

> The first paradigm shift pertains to where we, as the church, see ourselves in relation to our communities. Will we remain outside of the community inviting people in or will we go to our communities, seeking to be a transforming agent? The church is called to be separate in lifestyle but never called to be isolated from the people it seeks to influence. For many years founding pastor, Robert Lewis, of Fellowship Bible Church (FBC) in Little Rock was content to be growing a successful suburban mega church. By his admission, FBC was a "success church." Success churches seek to grow by having attractive programs and offerings that people can come to and benefit from. But Robert grew increasingly dissatisfied with the impact FBC was having on the community. So he made an appointment with the mayor of Little Rock and asked one question, "How can we help you?" The mayor responded with a list of challenges facing the greater Little Rock area.

> FBC then challenged themselves with the question, "What can we do that would cause people to marvel and say, 'God is at work in a wonderful way for no one could do these things unless God were with them?" That one question was the first step in becoming what Lewis calls a "bridge-building church." For the past four years, FBC has joined with over 100 other churches and over 5,000

25

volunteers in the greater Little Rock area and served their communities by building parks and playgrounds and refurbishing nearly 50 schools. They set records for Red Cross Blood donations and have enlisted thousands of new organ donors. They began reaching out to the community through "LifeSkill" classes (on finances, marriage, wellness, aging, etc.) in public forums like banks and hotel rooms, with over 5,000 people attending. In the past four years the churches of greater Little Rock have donated nearly a million dollars to community human service organizations that are effective in meeting the needs of at-risk youth. They have renovated homes and provided school uniforms, school supplies, winter coats, and Christmas toys for hundreds of children. After getting new shelving for her classrooms, one school principle said, 'I think this is the most fabulous day of my life as far as education is concerned. I've been in this 29 years and this is the first time a community or church project has come through for us.'

The churches of Little Rock have let their light shine in such a way that Jesus Christ is made real to the community. Once a church makes this mental shift regarding how it lives in its community, it is only limited by its creativity in how it can serve its community and be the salt and light it was meant to be. It makes the transition from providing ministry programs for the community to forever changing its relationship to a community. [9]

---

[9] Os Hillman, *Faith and Work Movement,* Aslan Group Publishing, Cumming, GA p. 105 2004

We see very few communities throughout the nation that have come together collectively to impact their city like the community of Little Rock has. In most situations, individual churches operate as silos in their communities. They do have some impact, but not what they could have if done as a collective Church of the city.

> *Serving the city is giving the Church more influence among its leaders.*

When all of these efforts become focused, the net result is we begin to fulfill Deuteronomy 28:13,14: "The LORD will make you the head, not the tail. If you pay attention to the commands of the LORD your God that I give you this day and carefully follow them, you will always be at the top, never at the bottom." In almost every case of the Church serving the city, the result is giving the Church more influence in the city among its leaders. This is biblical Christianity. We win by serving and solving problems in the community as a unified Body of Christ. Influence becomes a fruit of our obedience rather than a goal.

In April of 2007, I was led to begin a community transformation effort in my local community and city. Cumming, Georgia is a northern suburb about 40 miles north of Atlanta. The county population is about 125,000. This process started by a man calling me and asking me to meet with the pastor of the local First Baptist Church. This led to meeting two other pastors from two other denominations. The more we talked, the more we collectively began to build a vision for the city. Soon the Lord led me to some key intercessors who had a burden for the city. A core group of people began to form. We met for prayer two times a month, for noon to 1:00 PM every other Tuesday. We met in a historical schoolhouse located one block from city and county government buildings. Later meetings were held in local churches.

Several community vision casting meetings began the process of the blessing the city phase. However, the process is still young and growing in its development. There are many other communities that are farther along than we are. However, we understand the model that God has given us, and are walking as He leads in this process. (More information is on our website at www.PrayForsyth.com).

Community coalitions must begin through relationships of trust. Bringing together different denomination persuasions can be challenging. It requires laying down agendas, finding common areas of agreement, and having sensitivity to the differing expressions of faith. Charismatics must accept the more conservative expression of their mainline brothers and sisters. Mainline leaders must accept the more expressive Charismatic believers. God created all of us uniquely, and we must embrace one another for what we agree on, not what we don't agree on. A mentor once told me "doctrine is what you are willing to die for, everything else is negotiable." I believe he is right.

If we want to transform our cities, we must affirm the key role workplace leaders have in establishing the Church within the city by equipping them and validating their ministries through our local churches. We must be intentional about bringing intercessors, workplace leaders, and pastors who have a vision for their city together with an intentional process that allocates money and resources to projects that will bless the city. Then we will begin to see the transformation of cities.

A FINAL WORD

Joseph was a change agent whose life modeled the Kingdom of God. His secular employer saw God in him: 'Can we find anyone like this man, one in whom is the spirit of God?' Then Pharaoh said to Joseph, 'Since God has made all this known to you, there is no one so discerning and wise as you. You shall be in charge...'[10] Our goal is not to be in charge; our goal is to manifest the love and grace of Jesus Christ to all of the culture.

When we represent the Kingdom of God in our lives, we will naturally become change agents no matter where we reside. Are you ready to be a change agent for God's glory?

---

[10] (Gen 41:38, 39).

Os Hillman is president of Marketplace Leaders, an organization whose purpose is to help men and women discover and fulfill God's complete purposes through their work and to view their work as ministry.

Os is an internationally recognized speaker on the subject of faith at work. He is the author of 13 books and a daily email devotional called TGIF Today God Is First, which has over a quarter of a million daily subscribers worldwide.

Os' new book is Change Agent. He developed and teaches the Change Agent Intensive weekend training sessions, which is now available as a DVD Video Course. Os also helps lead a new initiative called The Change Agent Network. Os has been featured on CNBC, NBC, LA Times, New York Times, and many other national media as a spokesperson on faith at work.

Os is also president of Aslan, Inc. which provides a leading online Christian bookstore to serve the "faith-at-work" movement called www.TGIFbookstore.com, serving the needs of Christians in their workplace calling.

Os serves as Visiting Instructor at Regent's School of Undergraduate Studies (www.Regent.edu). He attended the University of South Carolina and Calvary Chapel Bible School, a ministry of Calvary Chapel of Costa Mesa, California.

3

LIFESTYLE MINISTRY BUILDING RELATIONSHIP: A PLATFORM FOR MINISTRY

by John Burkholder

What an awesome time we live in, and what an honor it is to be among the company of Believers of our Lord and Saviour, Jesus Christ. I often ponder if the Body of Christ realizes the significance of the hour in which we live: if we perceive that the whole earth is groaning for the manifestation of the sons of God; if we really know who we are as the church; if we know what the church is, what it should look like, and who and what Christians should be.

For so many of us, the church is the place we go to on Sunday mornings for service. We gather for songs of praise and worship, the dreaded announcements, and of course we would be remiss not to mention whether the pastor is going to finish his sermon in time for us to catch the game that starts in ten minutes.

> *To fully comprehend the awakening within the Body of Christ, we must acknowledge that we have been lulled to sleep.*

Some of us go because we are expected to. Is this really God's design for the 21st Century Church?

With all of my heart, let me respond with a resounding "no!" The church is in one of its most magnificent times of transition. There is a growing sense of frustration, discomfort, and agitation in the hearts of God's people. Lethargy and complacency are being called to a screeching halt by the power of the Holy Spirit. Our spirit man continually cries out with a deep yearning for greater dimensions of God with what seems to be an ever increasing hunger for more. We are not quite sure why and really do not understand, yet it presses upon our souls. We express dissatisfaction with thoughts like, "There has got to be more. Is this all there is?"

To fully comprehend the awakening of the Body of Christ, we must acknowledge that we have been lulled to sleep within what we call church. Religion, tradition, theologies, and eschatology have given us a cornucopia of reasoning for not simply being who we are called to be. In our sleepy state, God is awakening us. The alarm clocks are buzzing and chiming all over the earth and the Spirit releases a clarion call to arise!

The call to arise is an individual and corporate battle cry. The glorious sound of the revelry trumpet blows, and we the army of God are springing out of our cots, putting on our uniforms, and rushing out of the barracks of the church to gather in specialized battalion formations, each with an assigned, unique, and special mission. How great it would be that every saint is standing shoulder to shoulder with a fresh and new revelation of unity and rank compelling us forward through an inspired commonality and bond of purpose?

Each would be fortified in the knowledge that his or her capacity to march into the battleground of our own spheres of influence, as the sons and daughters the world is yearning for, is like no other. Each would be equipped with an experiential revelation that they themselves can move freely in the full manifestation of God's power and the demonstration of His love through the mighty expression of the Gifts of the Holy Spirit in complete operation. This would be the beginning of restoration, transformation, and reformation. Are you ready to rumble with the greatest army of saints ever assembled, to plunge the sickle in the earth for the greatest harvest of souls ever, as a prelude for Christ and the establishment of His Kingdom and eternal reign with all of us, His Bride, the Saints?

Understanding that we are in transition is necessary; more so, we must embrace that transition! As influencers in the Body of Christ, we must embrace the season of personal transformation first. The Holy Spirit is revealing where we are on God's time table and what He wants to do through us while we are here. God is connecting the dots of revelations, wisdoms, strategies, and timings for the implementation of God's plan for this hour.

UNDERSTANDING THE TRANSITION

One revelation we must apprehend is that every member of the Body of Christ has a sphere of influence and that no one can minister in that sphere as effectively as that individual can. The premise for that reasoning is that every person has a network of family, friends, work associates, classmates, and social affiliations through sports, recreational interests, and the like, all represented outside church buildings. The operative component is personal relationship. As leaders, we are being challenged to see beyond those that we serve within the context of ministry, and realize the very ones we are serving also have a captive audience of people, with various degrees of already established relationship within their own spheres of influence.

This is such an exciting scenario. Seeing through this new perspective is awesome. It causes us as leaders to recognize the capacity we have to reach so many others through the gifts, talents, and calling of our people, reigniting our passion and refueling our faith, hope, expectation and a love to see destiny fulfilled in the lives of others.

We are making great strides forward as the Body,... in unified purpose to see the Gospel demonstrated.

Equally exciting is the challenge we have to impart this revelation to every believer, empowering them with a personal conviction of their viable, pertinent role in the Body of Christ. Their passion must be ignited by God's purpose for their lives to fulfill personal destiny. What a win, win this is for all of us! As those we lead fulfill their destiny, collectively we fulfill ours, and the army of God garners a momentum to further advance the cause and purpose of this hour for reformation, ultimately co-labouring with the Holy Spirit to issue in the King of Kings Himself.

Once this revelation is received in the hearts of our own people, we will have the platform from which to train, equip, and activate the Saints in the working of signs, wonders, and miracles and the full expression and manifestation of the gifts of the Holy Spirit.

In this season, these components are beginning to unfold. Leaders are recognizing the treasures and potential of influence in their midst and shifting the Saints into position with revelation of purpose and destiny. We cultivate the revelation with the appropriate training and equipping. Now we have to answer the biggest question: how do we mobilize our people in their respective spheres of influence outside the familiarity of the church?

To begin with, let us look at the recent marketplace movements. "Marketplace" ministry has emerged tremendously within the Body of Christ. Truly amazing is that it has not been limited to a particular denomination or Christian persuasion; rather the "get outside of the four walls" saints are activating in the marketplace revelation exploding in a cornucopia of Christian expression. We are making great strides forward as the Body, not so much in unified theologies as much as we are in a unified purpose to see the Gospel demonstrated and manifested as the sickle for the harvest. Every Saint has a mandated purpose to fulfill!

I believe that in order to cultivate a greater momentum within the movement, we need to further disseminate the vision of "Marketplace" ministry and delegate it to everyday folks like you and me. The word "Marketplace" carries a connotation of business or the workplace. In its inception so many years ago, it was in fact launched through the gathering of business people. An awesome foundational platform has been established with these forerunners preparing the way for all the saints to actually begin to minister outside the restrictive mindsets of what the church should look like.

We should begin by redefining "Marketplace" ministry as "Lifestyle" ministry. Our commissioning in Mark 16:15-18 is to "Go into all the world and preach the gospel to every creature. He who believes and is baptized will be saved; but he who does not believe will be condemned. And these signs will follow those who believe: In My name they will cast out demons; they will speak with new tongues; they will take up serpents; and if they drink anything deadly, it will by no means hurt them; they will lay hands on the sick, and they will recover." Jesus is releasing a charge, the great commission, which is the responsibility of each of us to appropriate.

What exactly is "all the world?" All the world is all encompassing. All the world is indeed the Marketplace; however, it is also our families and extended families, our schools and their students, our sports teams and their team members, our dance studios and their participants, the cashier at our local grocery store, the multitudes in our local malls, the servers at our favorite restaurants, the attendees at our PTA meetings, the folks in our social clubs, support groups and the like, our neighbors, the person sitting next to us on the subway, bus or plane. "All the world" is every facet of our daily lives. It encompasses far more than the parameters of marketplace; it encompasses the everyday life of a particular individual and the opportunities they have to relate to those they encounter. Thus we pursue a new mindset of "Lifestyle" ministry.

We are not trying to change what is already effective but rather broaden our mindsets and expectations that the mandate is all inclusive, whether or not we have a place in the market. One of my favorite exhortations is that we are "ordinary people doing extraordinary things" with God! Our everyday interactions with others provide for us the opportunity to build relationships as platforms for ministry. Within the context of these relationships, and in conjunction with the Holy Spirit and our training, we can seize every opportunity to build relationship as a platform for ministry. Imagine an everyday lifestyle, in which every saint awakens daily with a resolute purpose, saying "here I am

> *We are "ordinary people doing extraordinary things."*

God, I am available to be used this day by you; to be your hands and arms, your embrace, your counsel, your wisdom, the facilitator of your healing and deliverance, the messenger of salvation, the worker of signs, wonders, and miracles, your encouragement, your hope, and your love!" Here in lies the quickening of the reformation and the re-facing of the church at large.

A PRACTICAL MODEL: THE BACK TO SCHOOL GIVE-A-WAY

My wife and I co-pastor a multi-cultural church in the inner-city of Buffalo, New York. Recently we had what we call a "Back to School Give-a-Way," where we gave away book bags and supplies to the children in our community. We have done this for years as an expression of the Father's love for all the children and to be His hand of blessing. As leaders, we do this event with purpose. Firstly, as a church family, we are doing what we are called to do according to the word, and secondly, we are providing a safe and controlled opportunity for our own church family to get outside the four walls of our own church, even if it is only ten feet out into our own parking lot, and put into practice their lifestyle ministry training, equipping, and activation.

Everyone has a part to play, and everyone has a personal revelation that Jesus has called them to do the same work that He did and even the greater works! Weeks before the event, we have our people scouting the "Back to School" sales, not just for good bargains but also with a purpose. You see our expectation is when they go into the various department stores, each one of them is an available vessel to be used by the Lord. Their search for supplies is an undercover assignment to forge relationship with whomever they can, whether that be the person next to them in the same isle, the cashier or attendant, or the person walking out of the store next to them. As the event date approaches, we assemble teams to sort and pack the book bags according to grades, ranging from pre-kindergarten to grades five and six. While doing so, they pray, releasing decrees over each bag and the respective student that will receive it. Decrees of salvation, healing, deliverance, protection, blessing, favor, breakthrough, restoration, reconciliation, acceptance, and affirmation, just to name a few, are spoken with an expectation to minister the love of Christ.

On the day of the event, we assign teams to various stations, such as the popcorn table, the candy floss table, the face painting tent, the prayer tent, and the barbecue tent. We gather and pray, and each team member anoints all the stations and all the book bags, which are now packed and ready to go. While at their station, each person remains ready to speak to and impact as many as they can, forging the type of relationship that provides opportunity to minister with the demonstrations and manifestations of God. Surprising as it may sound, in the aftermath of a great event, many of our church members felt challenged and stretched in their efforts to actually minister. The training and equipping of the saints is awesome! It is never without great joy that we see the saints come alive with an experiential revelation of moving in the expression of the gifts, whether it be prophecy, a word of knowledge, a word of wisdom, healing, or any other way the Spirit of God will move through them.

Interestingly, each church member can be taught and activated to operate proficiently in the gifts of the Holy Spirit within the church. However, when challenged to minister in the streets to complete strangers, it becomes a challenging adventure. The practicum of hands-on experience, without the comfort zone and familiarity of the church building, seems to be the missing link in our training of the Body of Christ. We are discovering that while people are trained up in the spiritual elements of ministry, they also need to be taught how to practically incorporate everyday life skills with the ministry of the Holy Spirit. This is how we ultimately minister through relationship and become that glorious church as a demonstration, manifestation generation of reformers.

Every believer has a unique sphere of influence, and our mandate as leaders is to train and equip believers to impact those spheres effectively, manifesting His love and power through the gifts of the Holy Spirit. For leaders, this revelation is fairly easy to grab hold of. In its simplicity, it is a strategic plan for your marketing force to cultivate centers of influence to create opportunity to market your products or service. We are not reinventing the wheel here; we are tapping into a basic "Market Place" stratagem where we cultivate our greatest strengths to maximize results. In order to do so, we need to help people be firmly rooted in their own personal conviction that they are carriers of something within them that other people desire and need: the Gospel, the Holy Spirit, and all that is ours through Christ. Secondly, we must equip them in how to tap into what they are carrying, essentially how to operate freely in the Gifts of the Holy Spirit. Subsequently, we must teach them how to "market" that which they are carrying so they can create opportunities to present it.

> *The knowledge of what we're offering is only a fraction of the equation. How to offer it is the biggest part.*

PASSION INTO PRACTICE

I learned valuable lessons and strategies about the difference between having passion and putting it into practice from some professional training I had early in my career. As a new representative, I was sent to the Head Office for weeks of hands on, intense training. We were inundated with product knowledge;

40

however, the biggest thrust of the training was the marketing. We were taught several different approaches to prospecting—how to canvass for an appointment by phone; how to utilize current clients to cultivate new marketing opportunities; how to canvass an unknown business or residential area within our districts by "cold calling"; how to write and target pre-approach letters; how to cultivate "centers of influence" within our families, friends, business associates, and personal relationships—all to create opportunities to market our products and services.

The knowledge and conviction of the products and services we were selling was only a small part of the equation. The "How to" was the biggest part. As the training progressed, we would practice each marketing approach in role playing sessions with each other. We would simulate phone calls, cold calls, and existing client calls, all with the objective to secure an appointment. Then we would role play the actual appointments with one another, taking turns bringing each other through the sales cycle of fact finding, creating and identifying needs or personal objectives, presenting viable solutions, and ultimately creating the desire to purchase with that glorious closing of the sale. I'm telling you that by the end of that intense training, I was going to set the world on fire. I could see my name on the top of the industry as an all-star producer. In my mind, I was already replacing my five year old car with a new Mercedes. Hey, nothing wrong with a whole lot of zeal and some good training—right?

Upon my arrival home, I immediately started my new career. For the first month, I was mentored by my manager. He was with me in all facets of the business and the field activation of my training. He would make a call, and then I would have to make a call. He would conduct an appointment, and then I would conduct an appointment. I am going to be honest with you. I was so scared and nervous to do what I had been so confident in doing within the safe surroundings of that Head Office and my fellow representatives, even with my manager with me. After a month with him, the calls and the appointments did become easier and I grew in knowledge and confidence. Oh boy, that Mercedes was looking real good by now. I loved what I was doing and really embraced the call to provide my services to others.

I will never forget my first day selling on my own. I arrived at the office around eight in the morning, planned my day, and was all ready to go out in the field by nine. Yet I was so scared to leave my office that I found every reason possible to delay my departure. I had to have my morning coffee, had to talk with the rest of the guys in the office, had to hide in the supply room, had to go to the lavatory (you know you can hide there indefinitely), had to run down and feed the parking meter so I would not get a ticket, of course taking the long way around a whole city block and stretching out the time. All this time, I was fighting the butterflies in my stomach, knowing that sooner or later, I actually had to leave the office. Finally, my manager came into my office at around eleven thirty that morning, and

> *The real test is when you break out of the familiarity and comfort of support to do what you have been trained to do.*

with great perplexity, asked "What in the world are you still doing here?" That was it. I had to leave. Well I would like to tell you that this Mercedes dreaming, set the world on fire, marketing representative hopped in his car and rode out to the his territory,

42

made several calls, secured several appointments and made three sales that day. Nope! I drove through my territory for the rest of the day. Around and around I went, until about four that afternoon, never once getting out of the car and talking even to one single human being. Instead, I decided to go home for supper.

I was qualified to do the job; I was highly trained by the best in the industry; I was mentored with hands on field training. The real test, however, comes when you have to break out of all the familiarity and the comforts of support to do what you have been trained and appointed to do. In the real world, as you can well gather by my own testimony, it is not always easy. Our own people, even with all of our training and equipping, all our mentoring and hands on examples in the "field," are still faced with the challenge of their first day in field all by themselves. I believe this is our critical point of reference in actually initializing and mobilizing the Body of Christ into action. It is bridging the gap between the equipping and the application.

This is where the crux of my own passion lies. I believe the missing link to all of our training and equipping of the saints is the how to integrate the use of the Gifts of The Spirit in the real world, the world in which each saint lives, their own spheres of influence. We all need a platform from which to minister the gifts. That platform is relationship. Relationship is the foundation of trust, wherein lies the open door for new frontiers of ministry. It is essential that we begin to teach strategic, practical life skills that will help the saints establish platforms of relationship with the objective to impact through the power and demonstration of God.

KEYS TO BUILDING MINISTRY PLATFORM
RELATIONSHIPS

There are key elements to "building relationships as platforms for ministry." There are a couple of basic truths that each saint needs to grasp to activate this type of training in their lives. First off, we must be fully aware that as we walk out our lives on a day to day basis, there is always somebody watching. Understanding that the manner in which we carry ourselves, our body language, our countenance, the way we speak, the way we listen and respond, the way we dress, our manners, the observation of protocols, and the extension of courtesy and etiquette all have within them the capacity to affect others. These have the ability to foster a safe personal place and create a bridge of trust. In Lifestyle Ministry Training, the understanding that somebody is always watching can motivate and empower us to utilize everyday life skills to create relational trust with those whom we interact, effectively creating opportunities to minister as the Holy Spirit leads.

The second, and equally as important, truth that we must activate is that God desires to use each of us. Jesus said, "Most assuredly, I say to you, he who believes in Me, the works that I do he will do also; and greater works than these he will do, because I go to My Father" (John 14:22 NKJV). God has given us our marching orders; it is time to break out of the four walls of the church and be the church. The reformation of the church has been decreed. Every Saint has a mandated purpose to be used by God. I can only begin to imagine what the church could look like with each believer fulfilling their purpose - now that truly is shouting territory! Imagining this apostolic reformation of the church is the easy part. The very notion that we can do the same works as Jesus did and even greater is amazing.

If we are to move and fulfill the mandate of reform, we must return to the basics of a one-on-one, intimate exchange with the people in our own sphere(s) of influence. I truly believe that without demonstration and manifestation, there will be no reformation. With all the new technologies and mediums of communication, it is very easy for someone to plug into some form of Christian programming, such as on TV or the internet. It is very easy to have Christian dialogue through email and the new social networking sites that are widely used by so many. There is now a global platform for the message of the Gospel. I want to challenge us all with this thought: Has this become a substitute for the hands-on ministry of Jesus Christ? Is there so much Christian programming accessible now that the lost and dying have become somewhat desensitized to it?

The world can easily "hear" the gospel; however, are they "experiencing" the gospel in an intimate, personal, tangible, and practical way? Are they experiencing the freedom of a prayer of deliverance; a face to face exchange with the love of the Father for them through a prophetic word spoken by another; or the miraculous manifestation of healing that makes the revelation of God real for them? If we are to bring reform, we must realize that the most effective way to bring reform is to introduce Jesus to the world through the demonstrations and manifestations of His word and that He will provide the undeniable and infallible proof of His love.

We must begin to ask of ourselves, "Are we available to be used of God today?" This basic availability provides us with a foundation to begin our training. Firstly, there is always someone watching. Are we going to use that knowledge as a catalyst to cultivate relationships for opportunities to minister with demonstration? Secondly, are we going to wake up every day with a desire to be used by God; are we willing to say at each relational juncture of our day, "Here I am Lord. Use me"? Are we going to present ourselves to the Lord today as truly available?

UNDERSTANDING THE PLATFORM

As we train the Body of Christ, we must teach the importance of knowing our environments and understanding the playing field. In the days of Jesus' ministry, He really did little ministry or miracles in the temple (the church). He did miracles among the people, places, and events He encountered in His everyday life. He ministered in the fields and countryside, He ministered in people's homes, and He ministered at the public wells. The same ought to be true for us. Our environments such as our homes and the homes of others, our place of work, the places where we go to do business such as the grocery stores, dry cleaners, hair salons, restaurants and the like, ought to be our fields of ministry.

My wife and I were on a cruise with another Christian couple who were also ministers. Every day, without exception, we encountered opportunity to minister. The ship and all the people in it represented our playing field. When we got home, we used all the different testimonies as examples of how we could move in the demonstrations of God outside the four walls of the church. About a year went by before we saw our friends again and we were sharing with them how we had been having so much fun sharing in our training sessions all the wonderful examples we had created with them in being the Church outside the church building. They laughed and said they too had been sharing everywhere they went.

They would tell people how much they had originally been looking forward to the cruise as a time of rest from ministry, yet the couple they were with always found opportunities to minister. They so wanted to just rest and relax, they explained, and they couldn't figure out why this was happening so frequently. Then about the fifth day into the cruise, while at breakfast, they got the revelation! Every morning, we would meet and have breakfast together, and every morning, I would ask the blessing before we ate. Well, don't you know that every day as part of my blessing over the meal, I prayed something like this: "and we thank you Lord that our steps are ordered by you today. We are available as your servants. Please, Lord, use us in any way that you would like. We thank you in advance for

We can go to work, or we can be released into the "harvest fields" as demonstrators of the one who sent us. The latter makes us the sickle for harvest.

all the wonderful opportunities to minister your love on your behalf." That day our dear friends interrupted my prayer and said, "John, would you stop praying that way. We just want to rest!" Oh, we all laughed so hard. I never did honor their request, and from two different perspectives as couples, we experienced together the awesome joys of being available and being used by God in the environment of a cruise ship.

47

One night while on the cruise the four of us met another family of believers. We were all standing in a lobby talking, laughing, and having a good time yet we did not realize that a man sitting on an open staircase nearby was listening and watching. Suddenly, he marched over to us and said "When I get off this cruise, I am going to kill someone!" Then he took off around the corner. Three of the guys went running after him, caught up to him, and talked with him. The man eventually gave his heart to the Lord and was saved. Glory to God! You see, his sister was married to a man who repeatedly abused her with physical violence. This man had determined he was going to take a cruise as his last vacation because he knew he would spend the rest of his life in jail after he killed his sister's husband. We encountered him the next day, and his countenance was beaming with joy. He proclaimed to us how much better he felt. He actually said he felt physically lighter. That man had a tangible, intimate, experiential revelation with God through the Holy Spirit. When we are available, God will use us!

Our work environment is another excellent relationship platform. We can either go to work or we can be released into the "harvest fields" as demonstrators of the one who sent us. The latter makes us the sickle for harvesting the very ones with whom we work. It could be that, in addition to the provisional aspect of our employment, our jobs and businesses are actually our cover for an undercover assignment from the Lord to manifest His kingdom in that environment! Our perspective makes the difference, and I believe we can change our perspective of the workplace.

Even our commute can be used creatively. My personal drive to the office is about twenty-five minutes one way. One day while traveling to the office, I passed a jewelry store of which I knew the owners. I asked the Lord if He had anything He wanted to say or do for them. Immediately, I heard the voice of the Holy Spirit say, "they are thinking of going left; however, they need to go right." After I asked the Holy Spirit what He wanted me to do with that word, He said stop in and tell them. So in simple obedience, I stopped and shared the word with them. The owner just said, straight faced, "thank you," to which I replied "you're welcome" and left his store.

About a month later, I spoke with them, and they explained how profound the word was for them and how the timing of it was critical. At that time, they were considering the acquisition of another jewelry store. After a significant amount of legwork, they were about ready to close on the purchase. Without warning, they were then approached with an opportunity to buy one of the most prestigious Men's Clothing stores in our city. What I did not know was that one of them had graduated with a Master's in Business and had worked extensively in that particular sector of retail sales and management. They were thinking of going left, the jewelry business, and the Lord said go right - the men's store. Subsequently, they made the decision to buy the men's store instead, and to this day, it is prospering and continues to bring greater viability for them and their businesses. Do we realize that being available in our day to day spheres of influence has destiny's potential in it?

A few weeks later, I was driving by their store again, and the Holy Spirit interrupted my thoughts, saying "no co-signer." I asked if that was for this couple, and he said, "Yes, call them and tell them," which I did! A couple of weeks later, I received a call from them, and they were ecstatic. They were in a business meeting with the bank that was going to finance the new clothing store acquisition and the meeting began to go bad. Apparently, there were concerns over some bad debt incurred from the previous owner and the bank was demanding a co-signer on the note. They were quickened on the spot by the word I had given and told the bankers "no co-signer." The meeting ended and the financing fell through. The very next morning they received a call from another financial institute that they had talked with in the process. They called to advise them that they would like to finance their purchase. No co-signer was required, and the bank gave them $40,000 more than what they had originally discussed. How cool is that? God desires to show Himself in a real and practical way in the lives of everyday folks like you and me.

SKILLSETS TO BUILD YOUR PLATFORMS

The whole concept of Lifestyle Ministry Training provides for us an awesome forum in which to connect the dots between the spiritual and the practical.

In our training, we teach the importance of manners and protocol in every situation. Since someone is always watching, our manners and our observance of proper protocol inadvertently help build the platform for relationships. People frame an opinion of us just on how they see us conduct ourselves. If you have ever gone to a wedding or formal event, you have probably been seated with people you do not know. Were you able to form an impression of them, either favorable or not, by the way the conducted themselves: their manners and their observance of the protocols of such an event? Don't be fooled; they did the same with you! The consistent execution of proper manners and protocols can garner both the respect and the trust of others who are watching at a distance. This has credence in both short term exchanges with others and in long term environments, like our places of work and places we frequent within our respective spheres of influence.

> *When people perceive you are sincerely listening, ...you will hear comments like 'I don't know why I'm telling you this.'*

Character, honesty, and integrity also can play an integral part in the building of short term and long term relationships. For example, have you gotten to the car after a trip to the grocery store and realized the cashier did not charge you for an item? Integrity and honesty dictates that you go back in to the store and right the error. I have had so many opportunities to minister on God's behalf because of the open door created by that particular situation.

At one time in my professional career, I worked in Supply Management for a world renowned agricultural manufacturer. My job had me interacting and interfacing between the "suits" in the office and the "workers" on the factory floor. As industrial environments can sometimes be, the dynamic with the plant floor workers was interesting to say the least. Being present in the midst of ungodly conversation was not unusual. After about four to six weeks, I noticed that when someone cursed in my presence, they would quickly apologize. After about three months, the conversation in my presence had completely changed. There was no cussing, no off color jokes, no perverse conversation.

Over a period of time, one by one, the plant floor workers would seek opportunity to talk with me alone. In these times, they would share intimate and personal things about their lives and families, providing ample opportunity to minister the divine counsel of the Lord. You need to know that not once did I say I was a Christian however, I believe that the character of Christ spoke louder than any words I could have spoken. Unknowingly, they were drawn to the presence of the Holy Spirit within me. Saints of God, we are just ordinary folks, and the manifestation of the glory of God shines through our vessels when we endeavor to walk uprightly before others. Walking consistently in Godly character, honesty, and integrity with revelation will provide countless opportunity to forge a bridge of trust and help build relationships as platforms from which to minister.

Additionally, in our training we teach on relevant appearance and presentation for various settings. What we wear, how we wear it, and when we wear it can have a direct impact in creating opportunity to minister. We also train on the importance of being culturally relevant. If we are going to be pursuing relationships and opportunities to minister then we need to become students of the culture. Instead of seeing our cultural and ethnic differences as obstacles we can learn about the cultures represented in our own spheres of influence as an opportunity to build relationship.

Our curriculum designates a significant amount of time in the areas of communication and listening skills. We teach and impart with understanding the art of conversation. It is amazing to see the liberty and empowerment that the saints can garner when they learn the simple dynamics of verbal and non-verbal communication. A smile, a pleasant "good morning," eye to eye contact, or a firm hand shake can all be effective tools of communication while creating instant opportunity. Equally important is learning what communications are appropriate and what are not. What our body language speaks and what it should not convey are all essentials of effective conversation. Teaching the dynamics of personal space and how to approach, enter, respect, and not violate it with those with whom we interact can help us communicate with greater efficiency.

Listening skills are equally important in building short and long term opportunities for ministry. Every one of us can learn to become a good listener. The process of good listening begins when we understand that everyone wants to be heard. Listening with purpose validates and affirms the person speaking. Have you ever noticed that when people perceive you are sincerely listening and interested in what they are saying, they often begin to share at ever increasing levels of personal intimacy and vulnerability? Then you will hear comments like, "I don't know why I am telling you this," or "I can't believe I shared all that with you." Becoming a good listener creates a safe and trustworthy environment. The validation of being heard creates a bridge of trust. Once again the presence of the Holy Spirit combined with our ability to operate in our spiritual gifts will always provide ministry opportunities.

Another exciting facet of our training is learning the dynamics of affirmation. Every one of us have an inherit desire to be affirmed. We can use this as a ministry opportunity by being in constant search for things to affirm in the people around us. Affirmation is not something that we just naturally know how to do; rather it is a learned behavior. We can very easily determine to look at others with the intent to find something good. We can decide that with every encounter we are going to see, through the eyes of the Lord, the seeds of greatness in others. My father once said to me, "Son in each person there is about ninety-five per cent good and five per cent not so good. It takes a real man to see the ninety-five per cent." That has stuck with me. It is so easy to see the not so nice things in someone else; however, with a disciplined approach to see the good in another we can cultivate an endless well of opportunity in which to affirm. Learning to live a lifestyle of affirmation with a purposed resolve to esteem, encourage, and build others has within it the potential to create opportunity to minister to anyone at any time.

By now you are getting the idea that our training must facilitate the revelation that each one of us, with purposed determination, can be available, utilizing everyday life skills in conjunction with the Holy Spirit to minister with demonstration!

At our home the garbage pickup is on Monday around 7:30 to 8:00 AM. I make it a practice to listen for the truck as it comes down our street. In the summer time I will have a couple bottles of water ready and when the truck approaches our home, I run out to greet the workers. I consistently tell them how much they are appreciated, strike up whatever small talk I can, and give them a cold bottle of water. One day when the garbage truck pulled up the man came to me asking if I could pray for him. He had received a bad report from the doctor that he had cancer. I readily put my hands on his shoulder and began to pray.

During the prayer, the Lord showed me a root of bitterness and unforgiveness in the man. After praying, I spoke with him in a very non-threatening and non-judgmental way about the importance of letting things go and the power of forgiveness. The he went on to do his work. I did not see him for quite some time until one day he was back on the truck.

When he got to our house he jumped out of the truck, ran over to me, and gave me the biggest bear hug ever! He was thanking me for my prayers and was filled with such a joy as he proclaimed out of his own mouth how God had healed him of cancer.

Who knew that the kind words of appreciation and affirmation along with a gesture of kindness through a cold bottle of water would lead to a miraculous supernatural intervention and healing of the Lord? Glory to God! This can and should be an everyday occurrence in the lives of God's own. The working of a life skill of affirmation and the gifts of the Holy Spirit are what it is going to take the church outside the four walls. That young man had a real life encounter with a living God, and that can never be stolen from him.

The simplicity of Lifestyle Ministry Training is in teaching the saints that they can be ministers of the Gospel and workers of signs, wonders, and miracles every day and every facet of their lives. We can truly be moving in both realms at the same time and must begin to incorporate the "how to's" of relationship building through operation of the gifts of the Holy Spirit.

One afternoon while in Florida for conference, my wife and I went to the mall. We stopped into a retail outlet store that sells all kinds of hats. We were greeted by a sales person in a typical friendly manner. I immediately engaged the young lady by asking if Jeff was still there. You see last year at that time, we were in the same store, and I had purposed to position myself as available to the Lord to minister to Jeff. Utilizing some basic communication, listening, and affirmation skills, I was able to strike up and maintain a significant dialogue with Jeff, forging relationship with him as a platform to minister. As it turned out we did not minister to Jeff that day, which sometimes happens, however I knew the next time I visited I could continue by referencing what I learned about Jeff that day. That point of reference was enough to engage our new sales person a year later. During our time of greeting, my wife looked at her, and with a twinkle in her eye, told our new sales person how "cheerie" she was and what a beautiful smile she had. In that short exchange between the three of us, by referencing a previous visit and releasing a word of affirmation, we built a bridge of trust and a door for ministry was created.

Immediately, with tears in her eyes, the clerk began to tell us how she had been through a very rough season. She had endured a major surgery, even showing us her scar, her mom was sick with cancer, and her husband was working out of town for extended periods of time. My wife engaged her and prayed for her, her marriage and her Mom right there in the store. While they were praying a couple of new customers entered the store. I greeted them and invited them to look around, ensuring them of my help should they have any questions. You see I took on the role of a sales clerk so my wife and the real sales person would not be interrupted. We were moving in complete harmony to ensure that that young lady had a real life encounter with a living God. Now that is what I call great fun with the Lord!

Our experience has shown us that one of the biggest hurdles we have in mobilizing the saints lies not in training them and activating them in the full expression of their gifts but rather equipping them with the knowledge and revelation of everyday life skill that empower them to defy fear and press beyond the comfort and familiarity of our churches and training centers. In doing so we can begin to release and activate the greatest reform the church has ever seen and the greatest restoration of the original church since that day of Pentecost with the empowerment and indwelling of the Holy Spirit. All power and authority have been giving to us, His glorious Church!

I believe the hour has come for us to once again be empowered with fresh revelation and a new charge from heaven. The time has come to bust out of the upper rooms and hit the streets. Why can't we minister to the person at the toll both on the interstate within a sixty second window of opportunity? Why can't we minister to our waiter at the local restaurant within an hour of dining? Why can't we minister to the sales person at the hat store in the mall? We can!

We are going to teach, train, equip, and activate the saints to bring the manifested glory and demonstration of God and at the same time teach and impart to them a set of life skills that they can learn to incorporate as a "Lifestyle." The two, knit together, launch the true faces of reform with a fire that spreads without limitation. The whole earth and everything in it belongs to our God, and the day is coming when we will stand with Him as the declaration goes forth that the Kingdoms of this world have now become the Kingdoms of our Lord!

John Burkholder worked professionally for over 20 years in Financial Services and Supply Chain Management and carries a passion to see the expansion of the Church into all facets of everyday life. He served as President of the Buffalo Niagara Chapter of the Community Impacting Business Network, a workplace ministry focused on the equipping of business people to forge impact in all aspects of their Marketplace endeavors. John and his wife Barbara have developed a "Lifestyle Ministry" Training Curriculum and travel throughout the U.S. and internationally, facilitating the training and activating of the Saints in the power and demonstration of the Gifts in their respective spheres of influence.

John is co-pastor and vision-holder of Sword of The Spirit Ministries in Buffalo, New York, an ethnically and culturally diverse inner-city church. He and his wife oversee a dynamic church of apostolic order, and have a mandate to prophetically impact the region through conferences and seminars as well as their School of Equipping.

John is a gifted preacher, teacher, and conference and seminar speaker with an accurate word for the Body, and a breakthrough anointing for business, healing, and deliverance. With a passion for prayer and intercession, he facilitates prophetic strategies for breakthrough, individually, corporately, and regionally.

John and Barbara are ordained with Christian International Apostolic Network under Dr. Bill Hamon and serve as Apostolic/Prophetic Regional Team Leaders for the CIAN New York/Ontario Region.

4

IMPACT THROUGH JUSTICE: THE RESPONSIBILITY OF COMMISSIONING

by Dr. Melodye Hilton

God continues to illuminate our minds concerning the remarkable mandate given us, individually and corporately, to establish His purposes within our spheres of influence—to be His voice and His hands, and demonstrate His heart of justice on behalf of hurting lives, struggling communities and divided nations.

I experienced a defining moment in my life years ago while on a pilgrimage to Edinburgh, Scotland. I visited the castle there and saw the beautiful crown jewels. I was confused when I saw a huge ordinary looking rock sharing an honored place adjacent to the crown jewels, all housed behind bulletproof encased glass. The rock looked so out of place, but as I read the inscription, I discovered it was the "Destiny Stone." It was upon this rock that the Kings and Queens would sit to be coroneted, at which moment

> *Tears began to run down my face because I recognized that to embrace destiny, I had to understand it's about first the Kingdom.*

"it was no longer about them, but their kingdom, their people, and their very land." To the people of Scotland, the Destiny Stone's wealth far exceeds money or prosperity.

Without understanding our divine directive, we would throw away that stone of destiny—our seat of Kingdom commissioning—for the more obvious beauty of the crown jewels, man's standard of success. We cannot ignore our most valuable inheritance and eternal purpose, though appearing common, by exchanging it for temporal wealth.

Tears began to run down my face as I stood looking at the crown jewels and the Destiny Stone, because I recognized that to embrace destiny, I had to understand from the heart that it was not about me, but FIRST the Kingdom—God's rule and reign manifested through truth, justice, and mercy. Secondly, it was about people! The question before me was, "Do I have a heart to see people redeemed, or just the land?"

Charles Finney embraced destiny submitting to the ultimate reign of God. He saw whole cities (people) come to Jesus, THEN the reciprocal to that was community transformation. Our core values cannot be about us personally, our business prospering, our church growing in numbers, or the revitalization of our towns and cities—though that is a by-product when the people in those cities are impacted by the heart of God! We cannot be caught up in the

"American Gospel" of comfort, goods, possessions, or the accolades of men; we must sit upon the Kingdom's destiny stone of commissioning through absolute surrender to God's core values and purpose.

As I have opportunity to provide corporate and governmental leadership consulting, my heart's cry is for God's heart to be imparted to those sitting around that table—I want them to see Jesus! Yes, I want to see prosperity come to their city and witness principles of truth change their corporation or nation, but only as seeds of redemption impact each individual life.

"Consciously or subconsciously we are always communicating something - what is our message?" Dr. Melodye Hilton

Though we may not evangelize in the traditional, religious sense, we are facing an open door to bring in the harvest. We teach Biblical principles using terminology that corporate and governmental leaders can understand. We speak their language; nevertheless, our motives, goals, purpose, and destiny is for the Kingdom of God to be manifested in their lives. We must serve our communities and the people by modeling the character of The One we serve.

"The moment you lean upon your title or position rather than the heart of service, your influence will weaken." Dr. Melodye Hilton

Dr. Bill Hamon writes in *The Eternal Church*, "As God limited Himself to the body of Jesus.....So has Jesus limited His contact with the world to His corporate body." We have this legacy to uphold!

63

God has chosen to plant us in a community and has surrounded us with people—a sphere of influence—to be living epistles read of all men. With a justice mindset, we will see the very land redeemed, wealth released, and a true demonstration of the Kingdom of God established.

UNDERSTANDING JUSTICE

Justice is the exercise and distribution of power, authority, influence, and wealth. That power is visible in the political and governmental areas, as well as in social, religious, cultural, family, educational systems, and in the marketplace. When we use this power to do good toward others, we become an instrument of justice. Sadly, when power is used to take from people what God destined them to have, that is injustice.

Sometimes life is just not fair, and injustice comes not through the hands of man but the circumstances of life. There is a literal enemy who hates God and those whom He loves—people![11] He is the ultimate instrument of injustice. Injustice flourishes in the midst of moral uncertainty, creating hot beds of fear, confusion, insecurity, and abuse, but God has planted us as instruments of His justice in our family, city, and nation.

In a world full of grey—where we are taught that truth is relative and you can even be your own god—many are desperate for a standard of right and wrong, for role-models that can be trusted, for pure motives without hidden agendas to be demonstrated. Our world is hungry to be loved, valued, and honored.

---

[11] John 10:10

"The human heart instinctively knows that it deserves justice. The human heart cries out for justice. However, our world is filled with injustice and suffering. The history of mankind is the history of injustice and abuse of our fellowman. It is the story of injustice, hostility, tyranny, brutality, anger, hatred, inhumanity, violence, and revenge..."[12]

Many say they desire to use their power and influence for good, but when it affects their standard of living or their popularity, they pull back.

The Word of God[13] is an absolute standard that will never lead us astray. Righteousness and justice are the foundation of the throne from which God rules and reigns.[14] There is a big difference between right and wrong, justice and injustice; our God is extremely impassioned about the difference. The Word of God says that He loves justice and hates robbery and iniquity.[15] He sees the oppression, the tears of the oppressed, and how power appears to be on the side of the oppressors.[16] Those who oppress the poor are insulting God![17] Believe it or not, the Bible says that

---

[12] Dr. Gary Allen before the United Nations in 1998
[13] The Holy Bible
[14] Psalm 97:2
[15] Isaiah 61:8
[16] Eccl. 4:1
[17] Proverbs 14:31

God hates the wicked and those who love violence![18] However, upright men—the instruments of justice—will see His face.

A sad reality is that many people do not carry a justice worldview. A worldview is a mindset, idea, a way of viewing things about yourself and your world that determines how you will live.

> *"What you value underlies all of your decisions and actions. It may or may not be a conscious choice, but it determines your future and how your life will impact society." Dr. Melodye Hilton*

Many say they desire to use their power and influence for good, but when it affects their standard of living or their popularity, they pull back because they do not want to be inconvenienced. *"The sad reality is that man's nature desires justice for himself, yet he denies it to others."* [19] This must change!

The Word of God tells us what is good and what is required of us, and that simply is—well, it is not so simple—to do justice, love mercy, and walk humbly with our God.[20] We are to defend the poor and the fatherless, do justice to the afflicted and needy, and to deliver them out of the hand of the wicked.[21] God is looking for His people to be a voice of justice for those who have no voice, His hands of rescue, bringing hope to the hopeless. Within us is the purpose and the tools needed to fulfill our part in releasing God's justice to a hurting world.

---

[18] Psalm 11:5-7
[19] Dr. Gary Allen before the United Nations in 1998
[20] Micah 6:8
[21] Psalm 82:3-4

We must diligently strive to make our young men decent, God-fearing, law-abiding, honor-loving, justice-doing, and also fearless and strong, able to hold their own in the hurly-burly or the world's work, able to strive mightily that the forces of right may be in the end triumphant. And we must be ever vigilant in so telling them.[22]

Many of us have experienced injustice, but the God of Justice has destroyed the works of darkness in our lives. Jesus' love has become a burning passion inside of us releasing us to be instruments of His justice!

Though we are not absent from the emotions of fear, we are courageously confident in the cause of justice. No longer are we bound by shame, resulting from who we are, where we came from, or the injustices against us—we know our purpose! Our willingness to leave our selfish ambitions and live for God will cause our voices to be heard when we speak for what is just and right.

We are called to impact the world like no other generation has done before us. We are desperate to live for a cause worth dying for. Transformation is stirring in our hearts, and justice is its name.

Do justice: and therefore fight valiantly against those that stand for the reign of Moloch and Beelzebub on the earth. Love mercy, treat your enemies well; succor the afflicted; treat every woman as if she were your sister, care for the little

---

[22] Grant, 'Carry a Big Stick' Page 121

children and be tender with the old and helpless. Walk humbly; you will do so if you study the life and teaching of the Savior, walking in His steps.[23]

DISCOVER PASSION AND PURPOSE

A justice life is relevant and applicable. One of the greatest mistakes we can make when reaching out to our communities is to try to replicate what another is doing. When we are stirred by others' testimonies, we celebrate knowing that God is no respecter of persons.[24] We must allow these testimonies to inspire our faith, but we must recognize that we have a unique purpose in God's Kingdom plan. *"To wish you were someone else is to waste the person that you are."25*

You and your organization have a God-given purpose. It is your distinct reason for existing at this time in history and the geographical location that you've been planted. We do not create our purpose; we discover it! We do not adopt another's passion, but confidently, courageously, and faithfully walk out ours.

"Walking in your purpose will take you from a life of success to a life of significance." Dr. Melodye Hilton

---

[23] Roosevelt 'Foes of our Own Household' Page 132
[24] Acts 10:34
[25] Unknown

It is imperative to discover the purpose birthed from the passion of our hearts, or we will live frustrated lives, always competing as we measure our success to another's—this is not wise.[26] Throughout our many years of pastoral experience, precious well-meaning saints would tell me and my husband about what the church down the street was doing or what sermon they heard or read in a book, trying to influence us to adopt another's God-given directive. Our answer was a celebration of what God was doing in and through others and an embracing of the truth taught by others, but with clarification of what God called our church to accomplish.

> *We are actually better together than we are separately, but each person must supply their unique passion and purpose.*

We must trust God to bring those who have shared values to partner in the family vision, rather than trying to build our numbers by keeping up with the most popular church in town or doing good things while obstructing our reason for being planted in the community. We must decide if we want to be successful in the eyes of God or in the eyes of man. This leadership mindset ultimately benefits those within our church family because our goal is to see them, as individuals, release their unique purpose.

Now, in balance, we must team with others of shared values in order to increase effectiveness. We are all a part of the body of Christ, and the whole body needs to function together synergistically, but it is also important that each individual part

---

[26] 2 Cor. 10:12

fulfills its unique purpose within that partnership. I want my brain and my heart to work in congruence, but my heart cannot fulfill the brain's purpose or vice-versa. We celebrate Kingdom alliances and partnerships because together we can accomplish more. Our local church has a corporate purpose in which individuals can release their unique passion and purpose in the midst of the whole. This then becomes a place of unified corporate vision with celebration and opportunity to release the individual.[27]

We are actually better together than we are separately, but the catalyst for this synergy is each person supplying their unique passion and purpose. True Biblical justice is when every hindrance is removed from your life in order for you to be (in Him) and do (for Him) what God has purposed. In the same way, our communities will experience true Biblical justice when hindrances are removed so they can fulfill their redemptive purpose.

Mine and my husband's ministry, from its very conception, is called to reach a young generation. My passion, which you now know, is justice—power used for good. My heart has always broken for the injustices against babies, children, and youth that have left identities distorted and their destinies thwarted.

Your passion is your internal GPS that leads you to reach out to those who are in desperate need of the passion you possess. Dr. Melodye Hilton

Your passion will supersede your desire for position, title, prestige, or power. It is more important to you than your own personal needs. It is that internal GPS that directs you towards

---

[27] Eph 4:16

your goals and objectives. It's your message, your heart, and your voice that cannot be silenced. You look for every opportunity to express that passion. My goodness, it is so strong inside of you that you will unreservedly sacrifice to see it released. You are actually energized the harder you work! Your passion is the place where you release the seeds to impact lives and communities—one person at a time, if necessary.

My passion for justice has led me to do some unusual things that many have not understood. For example, almost 30 years ago, the Holy Spirit spoke to me about the foundational years of life and how we, as a church, were to not babysit our newborns to three year olds, but to impart identity and destiny. The training and methodology was unheard of, but out of that was birthed a curriculum for the church and equipping tools for parents called, "Who's Teaching the Babies?"[28] Can you hear in the name the gentle pressure of my passion telling churches and parents, "You must teach your babies"? Passion carries with it such conviction that you are compelled to motivate others in that direction. This was an expression of empowering the church and parents to be instruments of God's justice in the life of the most vulnerable: babies!

> *Your skills are the tools that God gives you to release your passion!*

Many ask, "How do I release this passion?" The simple answer is, "Use your skills." Therefore, with the skill to train, I poured out my passion for justice leading to the establishment of

---

[28] "Who's Teaching the Babies?" Curriculum and Equipping Tools
www.WTTBabies.org

our school, the International Training Center.[29]   ITC was established to raise up young leaders to also be instruments of justice. I'm motivated to give them the "power of opportunity" to break off lies and limitations, and to develop within them a work ethic, acceptance of responsibility, and maturity. I long to see them arise and fulfill destiny and accomplish the plans and purposes of God for their lives. I long to see them go into every sphere of society as confident leaders as they release their God-given passion and purposes.

INTEGRITY OF PURPOSE OPENS DOORS OF OPPORTUNITY

Doors open when I am faithful to be who God has called me to be, living from the place of personal passion and purpose. Have you ever tried opening a door of opportunity that is invisibly dead bolted? It seems to be opening for others, but not for you! I want to impact my community, but my community doesn't want it. Lies begin to form that something is wrong with me; I'll never succeed, I'm not as good, talented, or anointed as another. What a horrible place to be emotionally and spiritually!

"I must make a conscious choice to determine my course of action and not stop until it is accomplished no matter my fears, my limitations, or the obstacles I face. Thus the process itself matures me." Dr. Melodye Hilton

---

[29] International Training Center, Elizabethville, PA www.GoITC.org

When I know my passion and am faithful to release it through the abilities given me, when I walk in my purpose no matter how ordinary it seems, when I refuse to compromise, remaining faithful, and when trusting God is evident in the midst of disappointment, hurt or betrayal—then at the fullness of time, divine connections will be made releasing opportunities. If we make the most of the opportunity to serve

As we value and apply natural principles, it will position us for a release of the supernatural.

selflessly and to be an instrument of justice—power and influence used for the good of others—we will see greater platforms of influence. Although the influence and impact in the beginning may be small in our eyes, we will see increase as we continue to honor God through our faithful expression of our purpose-filled calling.

Take a good look, friends, at who you were when you got called into this life. I don't see many of "the brightest and the best" among you, not many influential, not many from high-society families. Isn't it obvious that God deliberately chose men and women that the culture overlooks and exploits and abuses, chose these "nobodies" to expose the hollow pretensions of the "somebodies"? That makes it quite clear that none of you can get by with blowing your own horn before God. Everything that we have - right thinking and right living, a clean slate and a fresh start - comes from God by way of Jesus Christ" (I Cor. 1: 26-31, Message).

73

With all our efforts to touch the community, true impact has begun through the young people of our training center—a manifestation of my passion and purpose! All the aspects of leadership, justice, service, and work ethic are taught to our students, and they have the honor and privilege to model that before many. It is the students of our school who, for years, have empowered the success of the local YMCA's mentorship program for troubled young people. Going beyond our little community of 1,500 people, they have received awards and commendations from the county for their service. We've served large corporations in the state's capitol during events that impacted the entire region. We've led, participated, and served in many community projects for the police department, city councils, revitalization committees, local businesses, even individuals in need. ITC has request forms that anyone in the community can submit. These are all simple, practical, and natural manifestations of love, mercy, and justice.

> *"The supernatural created the natural; therefore, as we value and apply natural principles, it will position us for a release of the supernatural."* Dr. Melodye Hilton

When our students first served the city council in a small community near our school, people came out to watch them work. They thought they were juvenile delinquents doing a community service work detail only to find out they were kids from a little Christian training center down the road. It so stirred the people that they came out to work with the students. Through all these little natural and practical acts of service, we have been endeared to many, giving us the opportunity to be "salt" and "light."

Personally, my heart to equip young leaders of justice led me on a journey of personal leadership development as well as creating courses and materials to equip others. I simply was being faithful to my passion and purpose. One day a leader in our church had one of my leadership training manuals in her office at work. The president of this large and influential corporation saw it and loved it, which led to my first big corporate America consulting job, though I had already begun to invest into small business and business-minded leaders.[30]

JUST DO IT FOR ME!

Another defining moment took place a few years later when I was given the honor to train high level military officers. These were powerful and influential men and women not only from the United States but other nations. I was sitting in a small balcony around the room in which they were trained in the strategies of war. As I was waiting for these amazing leaders to arrive, I was nervously—more in fear than in faith—praying and wondering how in the world I ended up in that place; who am I to teach these highly intelligent and competent leaders? The Lord broke through my anxiety and said, "Melodye, I have more power than all of them put together." Well, of course, I knew that…in my head. "Melodye, I have more influence than all of them put together." Well, of course, I knew that too. Then my loving Father said, "Just do it for Me!" Instantly, all anxiety was washed away by the reality of why I was given this platform of influence. It was a revelatory moment that brought simple truth from head knowledge to a heart reality. Just do it for Jesus for His Kingdom! I could do that! I could do it with full assurance knowing that my Father would be pleased! I knew if I gave my all, fulfilled and released my purpose and passion, I would be able to impact their lives for good.

---

[30] Dr. Melodye Hilton, consultant www.DrMelodye.com

My passion for justice—power used for good—and my unique methodology of leadership has impacted community, business, governmental, and educational leaders worldwide. What stirs my heart even more is the honor that God has given me to communicate the heart of my God through word, deed, and spirit! These are platforms and opportunities that traditional ministry would not have given.

NO MORE EXCUSES!

The skills that God has given you, the passion within, and the motivation to release it is not the responsibility of another—it is your responsibility. God will use others to give you the power of opportunity, but only you can make the most of that opportunity! There is no time to make excuses why you cannot be successful in impacting lives or communities. Every life you impact, impacts the family and community in which they live. Every mountain of society is not about high level institutions and structures, but it is about individuals that function within those mountains of influence. The mountain of the Lord's house will be exalted above every mountain of society - one person at a time![31]

Shame—a false identity that screams lies to us about our value—often tries to drive us to accomplish the world's or man's view of success.[32] It must be big money, power, prestige, high positions, international visibility, etc. It tells us, "If I do big things in man's eyes, I must be good, valuable, and important!" The fact is, greatness simply is obedience to our Lord, Master, and King.

---

[31] Isaiah 2:2; Micah 4:1
[32] Double Honor: Uprooting Shame in Your Life by Melodye Hilton

We are building His Kingdom of which we are stewards and partakers.

If our eyes are on the grandiose, the opportunities that make others applaud our accomplishments, then we are missing the simplicity of our commissioning to go into all the world.[33] As we sit upon the "destiny stone," it is no longer about us, but about the Kingdom, the people, and the redemption of the very land. We must see greatness in every act of obedience to the Lord. We must see value in and celebrate the unique passion and purpose given to us by our God, whether it appears small and unseen or is visible to the masses.

In 1982 my husband and I were commissioned by the Lord to move from Kansas City, Missouri to a little town in the Appalachian Mountains of Pennsylvania. I felt angry and frustrated. I had a city mindset and didn't want to live in rural America. I loved diversity of cultures, and we were placed in a white German community that didn't want "outsiders," of which we were one. I had every reason to make excuses why we could not succeed. I could blame the area, the people, the mindsets, the limitations, the continual rejection from the people we were sent to serve—and I did! However, through the years, I made a decision to trust my Lord, celebrate the land in which we were called, and just be faithful. I made a decision to simply be obedient and

> *When you value something, you will protect it, invest into it, sacrifice for it.*

---

[33] *kosmos*-order, government, the land, the inhabitants, world affairs, total of all things on the earth

pleasing to the Lord. I repented for speaking stout words against God through the hidden complaints of my heart.[34] I repented for the lie that it was vain to serve God, and that it could not bring profit to me. I made a decision to celebrate and honor God's plan, to allow Him to heal me of my life's shame, and just be faithful.

"Vision stirs value, and when you value something or someone you will protect it, invest into, sacrifice for, and treat as valuable." Dr. Melodye Hilton

My mindset changed from, "We are in the middle of nowhere!" to "We are in the middle of somewhere." It is not the size of the town, but the size of the vision, and you can reach the world from anywhere. I began to value our commission, motivating me to value the precious people and the little town surrounding us—the place of our destiny fulfillment. Now, years later, we are reaching the world from this little community!

"The problem is not ability, but the attitude and subsequent emotions concerning our responsibility (response to ability)." Dr. Melodye Hilton

We can no longer try to be what we are not or live in comparison with those we view as successful, but be faithful to who we are. Biblical attitudes and truth-based emotional perceptions are the links to the successful response to the abilities given us. From a sincere heart, we must be faithful in the little…period! The little given through a pure heart will multiply

---

[34] Malachi 3:13-16

according to God's divine purpose, knowing that He is looking for faithful stewards to whom He can entrust authority.[35]

BE CONFIDENT IN GOD'S PURPOSE

Your passion and purpose helps you to make decisions that align with God's plan. If your affirmative choices align with God's purpose for you, you don't need to spend hours in prayer to release that purpose. You are just faithful to what He's given. Longing to be in the center of God's perfect will is the easiest way to stay there, for He is the author and the finisher of our faith.[36]

We soon learn where to focus our time, efforts, and energy. We are empowered to follow-through to completion on a task because it is birthed out of confidence. We hold steady our course in the midst of challenges, disappointments, and apparent failure. It allows our "yes" to be yes, and our "no" to be no.[37]

We are God's creation; He placed within us the ability to have dominion and steward what He has entrusted.[38] So it is safe to conclude that as long as we love our God with all our heart and love those He loves, we can take what He has given to us and give it away—that is a manifestation of His justice on behalf of others.[39] Your community needs what God has planted inside of you. You are a key to someone's eternal purpose!

---

[35] Luke 19:17
[36] Heb. 12:2
[37] James 5:12
[38] Gen. 1:26-28
[39] John 13:34-35, John 15:12, 17; Rom. 12:10; Rom. 13:8; Gal. 5:13; 1 Thes. 3:12

But as touching brotherly love ye need not that I write unto you: for ye yourselves are taught of God to love one another (I Thes. 4:9).

We don't need a "thus saith the Lord" to do the revealed will of God, fulfilling His commission. Once I had clarity and could articulate my passion and purpose—my unique role in the body of Christ—I just used my sanctified decision making ability to make the most of every opportunity that aligned with that. However, there are times when I am moving in a direction that fits me, and the Spirit of God gives me a "red light," or a "don't go there," and I simply obey. If I do not have a constraint from the Holy Spirit, and it fits my passion and purpose, I just do it!

GOAL OF COMMUNITY IMPACT

God does not only have the ability to love, He IS love! God's emotions, passions, and what makes Him angry or brings joy to Him is birthed out of His purpose—love! When our hearts and actions align with His purpose, we will be able to unlock and open up, one step at a time, our community. When our uniqueness is released to others and our communities, we will see God's Kingdom released.

We have been commanded to love others as He has loved us. The foundation of the word command carries with it the meaning to continue in because of the aim and purpose of the one commanding.[40] Success will always be the by-product of our

---

[40] *entellomai,* meaning: to order, command to be done, join with; the foundation of command, *telos,* carries the meaning of: continue in because it is the aim and the purpose

attitude, motives, and purpose aligning with God's ultimate purpose.

You have been commissioned to fulfill God's purpose through releasing your purpose in your sphere of influence. Be true to God and true to yourself. No longer compare yourself, your standard of success, or your value based upon the works of another. If your heart is for justice—power and influence used for the good of others—and it's conceived and birthed out of God's love, what you do, large or small, for one or for many, will impact your world in a powerful way, establishing God's Kingdom.

Dr. Melodye Hilton works with individuals and workgroups around the globe as a Leadership Consultant and Behavioral Analyst. Through years of leadership experience and human resource consulting, she has developed a unique and personal approach to creating a sustainable and positive impact within her spheres of influence.

Her recognition extends over all generational, socio-economic, and educational backgrounds through her work in corporate and local business, government, and public and private educational sectors. She has served as Vice-President of a not-for-profit corporation for over 30 years, founded the International Training Center for the development of young leaders, and has a passion to see individuals and teams discover purpose through developing their full potential.

Dr. Melodye has established the Voice of Justice Foundation to provide scholarships, nationally and internationally, for potential young leaders to receive training, aid in the rescue and care of orphans and children in developing nations, as well as partnering with other organizations to impact a generation with hope, vision, and purpose.

For more information: www.drmelodye.com

5

PEOPLE NOT POLITICS

by Jon McHatton

In just six years, the civic nonprofit organization CARE INC, which aids local leaders around the world in improving their communities, has established itself in three nations, eight counties, and many more cities and towns. CARE INC has earned awards and acclaim from government, business, nonprofit, and faith leaders for developing programs and relationships whose "Best Practices" impact their communities. The following is the brief history and highlights, How to's, and Best Practices achievable when government and faith leaders focus on people, not politics or religion.

THE BEGINNING

In 2003, I received a phone call while sitting at my desk being a "good" pastor of a small but extremely busy church. "I am considering running for Governor, and someone on my staff suggested I call you for prayer." The man went on to say that he was a former Congressman who found Jesus as his Lord and

> *The mayor asked, "How can you serve the people of my city?"... I felt all that I have inside of me challenged.*

Savior while serving in Washington D.C. Feeling a sense of spiritual destiny and utter bewilderment, I said, "Yes" and scheduled the appointment. The result was twofold: a lifelong friendship with a brother involved in high levels of International, National, State, and local government, and me stepping into what was spoken over me during my commissioning at Christian International, "You are called to be a gatekeeper in government."

As a result of this phone call, I became the prayer partner for my brother, I became Chaplain of the State Legislature, and I gained access to every government official in the State. Meanwhile, I started a civic nonprofit corporation called CARE INC. Why I chose civic and not religious, God only knows! I had never heard of "Civic Nonprofit," and the CPA who helped me form the corporation had never filed an application with the IRS of this nature. I simply knew that I needed a vehicle that allowed me to work with all faiths, all political parties, and all government officials. This choice became a key stone in the development and success of funding and community collaboration.

In 2005, sitting in the Legislative Chaplaincy Office at the State Capitol, I began thinking and praying about how I could better serve the legislators and the people of my State. Meeting with the legislators and staff, facilitating conflict resolution seminars, delivering the prayer before opening session was an honor, but I felt there was something more for me to do. I was impressed with the urgency to get to know the people whom the legislators represent. I knew I needed to begin to meet with Mayors, another key stone to community impact.

I started the process by meeting with the Mayor of the city where I live. He was new in his role, so I asked my "brother" in government to go with me, just in case. They had a mutual respect for each other, so the meeting was scheduled and initiated on a high level of acceptance. Because I was a pastor and the Chaplain of the Legislature, the Mayor expected "prayer" or that I was going to ask him to engage in some religious exercise. However, I was there for another reason. I wanted to know how I could better serve at the Capitol by learning his perspective of the city's need. The Mayor stated, "I will pray with anyone who will show their faith through service!" My response was, "What is your passion, and how can I serve you?" This is the question that I knew I was to ask the Mayor and the only direction I had previous to the meeting. The Mayor replied, "I don't know…I have never been asked that question!" The next question was another defining moment in the process of community impact. The Mayor turned the tables on me when he asked, "How can you serve me and the people of my city?"

This question is particularly apropos for someone who has been trained and encouraged to hear the voice or leading of God at all times. I felt challenged; I felt all that I have inside of me challenged. I knew to center the answer on convening the Faith Based Leaders to meet with the Mayor. The Mayor agreed, and we began the journey now known as For Our City.

ANOTHER DEFINING MOMENT

In 2008 I convened a first-time meeting of mayors and faith-community leaders from a particular county. After introductions, a pastor asked, "Can you tell us, Mayors, what do your cities need?"

The host Mayor replied, "That is rather humorous that you asked us this question, because we were going to ask you the same question."

Every leader is looking for their life and efforts to have significant impact, but each must lay down his or her individual desire to achieve it.

Surprised laughter ensued as everyone realized that our agendas and expectations for the meeting were way off the mark. We were seeing that the other person or influential sector had the answer rather than perceiving that the answer is in all of us collaborating, strategizing, and then implementing solutions. We all, working together, are the solution we need. It is in cooperation and collaboration that we strengthen the community. As we work together, we become the answer to the individual, difficult questions. It was a defining moment for CARE INC. It made our mission clear.

What happened after was the beginning of what has made For Our City so unique and successful: "Table Talk."

A FEW NOTICES FROM THIS MEETING

Instead of the Mayor or City taking the lead, everyone in the room stepped into their leadership spheres. Individual leaders understand "perceived need." Identifying the actual needs of the community required multiple perspectives from many leaders. The Mayors knew the fiscal budgets, crime, and social service statistics and the "Master Plan" of their cities, while the Pastors and leaders of faith knew the stories and the people's needs.

Redefinition of terms in order to assess the actual need was essential in effective collaboration. "City" became "people" as "Church" became "people." Every sphere has interaction with people on different levels, and the goal is to come as leaders of the "City/people," identify resources, and discover what we can do better together than separately.

Every leader is looking for their life and efforts to have significant impact, but each must lay down his or her individual desire to achieve it. Significant impact takes the celebration of all logos, championing everyone's success and dropping all egos. This creates a safe "incubator" to dialogue for solutions that eventually identify overlapping resources and efforts, which leads to maximizing services and program impact in the community.

This helped create a model of Community Impact called "For Our City."

ALLOWING THE MAYOR TO SET THE AGENDA

A Mayor called me asking if he could meet to speak with me about a need he had in his city. He was very troubled, so we

87

scheduled the meeting that week. The need was that the city was suffering after a murder in the park. This was a close knit community that did not experience a lot of violence, let alone a homicide.

He asked me what we could do to bring healing to the community. After a brief discussion, we decided to launch For Our City with a "Healing of the City" Mayor's Breakfast. The suggestion was made to make it a "Prayer Breakfast," but even though there is prayer at For Our City, the focus is on service and unique ideas for the community.

The event was the most successful breakfast to date in that city. Prayer was given and leaders from every sector discussed needs and opportunities to eradicate one of the reasons for the murder, homelessness.

With this discovery, the Mayor and Host Committee formed a task force to research Best Practices for portable and low cost housing. A social service organization also stepped up to give temporary assistance to the homeless. A For Our City Director from a different city was attending and offered a Best Practice they have modeled with the faith community that opens their churches and synagogues to house and feed the homeless for the night.

The healing came as a result of leaders coming together to serve, putting feet to their faith, and taking the talk from the table to implement it on the street. To this day, there has not been another homeless homicide in that city.

The unique characteristics of the For Our City model:

1. ***Forming a Host Committee co-hosted by the Mayor and For Our City Director.***
   So many issues and emotions associated with the needs of a community can easily derail a community leadership collaborative. Identifying and serving the passion of the Mayor provides a stable and consistent focus while the Host Committee provides the administrative, communication, and marketing support. Both the Mayor and leaders working together also gives an opportunity to identify some of the cultural and long standing judgments and relational hindrances, and allows the Director time to bring healing to the few to bring change to the community. The reality is that when the Mayor invites leaders to a meeting, they come.

2. ***Host Committee is made up of all four sectors of leaders: government, private, public, and faith based.*** Even though seven mountains have been identified and well marketed, the American society utilizes four sectors to identify the cultural groups of collaboration and influence. All transformational community solutions require the resources, talents, and paradigms of all sectors. Each sector of influence is not sufficient but all of them together produce a synergism comparable to the principle of the building of the tower of Babel.

3. ***Breakfasts are used to convene leaders in a "safe place."*** It is a well-known fact that the best way to convene leaders is to feed them. The other less known fact is that leaders need a "safe place" in order to collaborate. This is not based upon the location but the way the breakfast is managed. It is not the large things but the small details. Name tags are first and last name, without title or organization. This enforces the need for communication between leaders before and during the breakfast. Another detail is to have pre-registration so that the Director and Host Committee can assign the leaders seating to assure all four sectors are represented at each table. One last detail that helps the leaders comfort and effectiveness of the event is to have the Host Committee serve as table monitors. This brings an extension of the Mayor's authority and focus to every   table.

4. ***Create a level playing field.*** Most cities base their collaborative efforts on information sharing of events and opportunities. This entails one sector dictating and managing the effort of communication and networking. For Our City is based upon a multi-sector assessment, strategy, and implementation for solutions. The need is assessed and agreed upon first. Then the need becomes an opportunity to find or create a Best Practice that is self-sustainable in three years.

5. ***Celebrate all logos and drop the egos.*** Identity is very important to the leader's mission and purpose.

The logo represents these things and should be celebrated. Many times there is a fight or competition that appears to be egocentric, when it is actually an identity crisis or a limiting of expressing passion. The celebration of the leader's identity creates an environment for what we can do better together than separately.

6. ***Assess and celebrate the current service activities from organizations.*** Closely akin to celebrating all logos is the assessment of what the organizations are doing in the community. There are great things being done by all of the four sectors. The problem is that the leaders do not know what each other are engaged in. When everyone participates in the assessment, value for one another grows and the opportunity to collaborate is established.

7. ***Establish task forces for research to form suggested solutions.*** A task force is made up of a few Host Committee members who have the desire and expertise in the focus area. This group of leaders will do the research that helps the main purpose of identifying a "base line" to set measured outcomes for sustainability. This think-tank also discusses strategy and options that would achieve the outcomes in order to report back to the Host Committee.

8. ***Identify and maximize overlap of resources and efforts.*** One of the major needs in a community is the waste of resources and doubled efforts. The

91

first step in this resolving this is identifying organizations that have the same passion and mission. This leads to an opportunity for the organizations to make a choice to collaborate or schedule their events to extend services to the community. One example is instead of the city having 30 Thanksgiving meals on one day, they are feeding once a day for 30 days in November.

BEST PRACTICES AND SUCCESS STORIES

HURT – Holistic Urgent Recovery Training.

At one of the For Our City Breakfasts, the Chief of Police and Fire Chief made the statement, "for the first 72 hours, you are on your own. We will not be there for you!" They went on to say that their responsibility is to restore critical infrastructure for the city and manage chaos. In hearing this, the Host Committee decided to develop a training program that trains people to take care of themselves and family members in emergencies. Not wanting to reinvent, we researched FEMA materials and found an Independent Study that was rather exhaustive and difficult to teach. As a result, HURT was created. This is a concise "train the trainer" program to which faith communities can add their faith principles. Christian Emergency Network has taken the HURT program and added their "Biblical Readiness" training incorporating it into the Ready Christian program. The HURT program provides Internet support, PowerPoint and teacher's guide, student manual, resources to assess faith and nonprofit organizations readiness, and tools to maintain individuals in Emergency preparation for the first 72 hours of crisis. The designers are from the Police and Fire Departments, EMS, faith community, and Citizens Corp. It has become the initial access program for (CERT) in the Citizens Corp of Central Arizona and Christian Emergency Network.

COMPEF – Community Preparedness Exercise and Fair.

Community Preparedness Exercise & Fair mobilizes community organizations and volunteer citizens in collaborative preparation for emergency situations in which urgent and immediate response is required for holistic recovery. The event entails a Preparedness Exercise: coordination of community organizations and emergency preparedness trainees to establish a network and communication system, mobilizing quick and effective response to a crisis in the community. The event also includes HURT Facilitators Training, a 72 hour emergency kit display, a blood drive with Red Cross, a food and clothing drive for the homeless population, and exhibition of emergency

> One of the major needs in a community is the waste of resources and doubled efforts.

and health related service organizations. This program is considered a Best Practice by Arizona Citizens Corp, County Emergency Management, and local Fire Departments.

Citywide Drives: Backpacks, Food, and Toys.

In one of the first For Our City Host Committee meetings with a Mayor whose passion was volunteerism, the Mayor asked the assembled group of leaders what their organization was doing for the community. One leader raised her hand and proudly stated that her organization recently held their 15th annual back to school backpack drive. "More backpacks were distributed than ever before!" and then someone else raised their hand to report that they too completed their most successful backpack drive. Then another, and another and another; by the time everyone finished reporting, there were nine organizations sitting at the table who had backpack drives, the same day in the same community. The Mayor began to chuckle, pushed his back from the table and laughingly said, "I can see a kid in his room with nine backpacks, wondering how he can sell eight of them." Fast-forward three years and that city now has five distribution areas for backpacks with communication and collaborative management between the sites. The result is serving more people with more resources by Maximizing Overlap of Resources and Efforts. This Best Practice has now impacted adjacent cities that are now doing similar collaborative projects, including receiving and distribution centers.

Project 85281.

During the assessment process in one of our partner cities, the taskforce found a particular zip coded area was impoverished. What made this more intriguing is that the area also housed the cities financial district, including the Chamber of Commerce and residence of the Mayor. This revealed the fact that there were pockets of poverty and areas of affluence in 85281. Project 85281 focuses on the vast needs of an area estimated to be the second highest poverty level and lowest income level in the county. Project 85281 seeks to raise awareness, mobilize volunteers, and strengthen the programs already serving this area of the city. The collaboration is extensive in order to eradicate the need and transform the neighborhoods. Some of these partners represent a major University, Chamber of Commerce, Police Department, multiple Municipal and Nonprofit Agencies.

CARE INC is an example of the synergistic, powerful effects when a community works together. When the church cooperates with the government and marketplace to meet the needs of the community, God's Kingdom advances forcefully. CARE INC works effectively in many communities around the world. Like other effective community transformation initiatives, CARE INC was birthed from the vision and passion God placed inside one person. God has placed similar vision and passion inside every member of His Kingdom. Yours may have another name. It may establish its own "Best Practices," its own vision, its own function. But yours exists. Yours is waiting to flourish!

THE IMPACT CONTINUES

Annually, Neighborhoods USA (NUSA), a national non-profit organization committed to building and strengthening neighborhood organizations, recognizes outstanding programs implemented to improve neighborhoods by a governmental entity, business, or corporation. In 2012, For Our City Chandler has been chosen as a finalist for the 2012 Best Neighborhood Program of the Year Award.

Let's Pull Together is a volunteer fueled effort to clean up properties overgrown with weeds. Initiated in 2010, the program serves as an opportunity for volunteers to help those who may be unable to work in their yards, such as senior citizens, disabled residents, and foreclosed properties.

During the fiscal year 2006-07, the Neighborhood Resources Division received more than 1600 complaints regarding weeds. By the end of 2009, the City of Chandler received over 2,600 weed complaints. The high number of calls was due to the decline in the housing market and the rise in the number of foreclosures. One morning, at a For Our City Chandler meeting, community representatives sat at a table to discuss the number of complaints that the City was receiving. During the meeting, someone exclaimed "Rather than complain about it, why don't we just pull together!" What a wonderful idea!

Let's Pull Together is about Calling your Community to Serve. Chandler declared its war on weeds through a Press Release issued on April 21, 2010 to the community of approximately 240,000 residents, asking them to call the City's Neighborhood Resources Division with addresses of vacant properties and any phone numbers posted on the properties. The citizens look for the weeds, call it in to the city, the city verifies, contacts the owners, and assigns the tasks to For Our City. Additionally, residents and service group organizations were being asked to assemble volunteer teams for a weeklong battle against weeds beginning April 24th through May 2nd. One of the largest obstacles was getting authorization from banks and past homeowners to allow volunteers access to the yards of vacant homes. During this time, many cities throughout the nation felt defeated by weeds because it was unclear as to who had jurisdiction over a property in the midst of a foreclosure. Obtaining any cooperation from banks and/or homeowners was a tireless and frustrating task. FOC and the City of Chandler took on the challenge in an effort to regain its beautiful, vibrant neighborhoods once again. In one weeks' time, approximately 90 volunteers assisted with phone calls to obtain authorizations for removal of weeds, trash, and debris off vacant homes throughout the City.

Let's Pull Together is about Networking. On April 20, 2011, a Press Release was issued asking residents once more to Pull Together to fight the war on weeds. Neighborhood Resources reached out to over 1,100 neighborhood leaders that represent over 280-registered neighborhood groups in both HOA and traditional neighborhoods. In addition, the event was publicized through the

96

Mayor's Listening Tour, which board members, homeowners, and young leaders attend five times per year at local elementary schools, and through the HOA and Traditional Neighborhood Academies. For Our City Chandler requested volunteer support in their newly developed For Our City Newsletter, specifically intended for distribution to the Chandler Unified School District, Chandler/Gilbert-Community College, nonprofits, and faith-based and service organizations.

The City's Code Enforcement Division also played a significant role by identifying areas requiring weed removal and leaving friendly door hangers on owner occupied homes that were in violation of the City's Code.

This year, and as part of Chandler's Centennial Celebration, Let's Pull Together was extended over the course of two months to provide just another way for Chandler families to meet the 100-Hour Volunteer Centennial Challenge, attaining 1,000,000 hours of volunteer service. The door hangers asked residents to Pull Together with their neighbors to remove weeds from their yards during the 10-day citywide weed pulling effort. This year, two neighborhood groups were inspired to organize, because Let's Pull Together offers an opportunity to meet a neighbor while cleaning up a neighborhood.

Let's Pull Together is an excellent example of city impact through cooperation. Let's Pull Together demonstrates exactly what community impact is all about. Let's Pull Together is about

- Connecting People
- Building a Stronger Community
- Making a Difference
- Connecting Neighborhoods and an
- On-going Commitment to the Community

97

**Jonathan McHatton** has been in Community networking and ministry for over 30 years. He has established Businesses, Community Programs, Churches, and Ministries. He has assisted in mobilizing Community Health, Wellness, and Fitness Clinics with continued Life Wholeness Training.

Jon has also established "For Our City," a strategic opportunity for Civic, Business, Nonprofit, and Faith leaders to collaborate for community transformation. "For Our City" is in six counties and ten municipalities in Arizona.

He has assisted in the developing and networking an Emergency Response and Recovery Program called H.U.R.T (Holistic Urgent Recovery Training) and COMPEF (Community Preparedness Exercise Fair) under CARE INC, (a civic 501 (c) 3), of which he is founder and President (www.care-inc.org). He has also helped to establish Community Citizen Corp Councils and served on the Arizona VOAD Executive Council.

Jon is the former Chaplain of the Arizona Legislature and Field Director for the Christian Emergency Network. Jon is an author and publisher, and is ordained, along with his wife Kim, under the Christian International Apostolic Network.

6

ENTERING GOD'S REST: WATERSLIDE CHRISTIANITY

by Rich Marshall

"Therefore, since a promise remains of entering His rest, let us fear lest any of you seem to have come short of it"(Hebrews 4:1).

Shortly after the January 2010 earthquake in Haiti, I found myself on the way to that devastated country. The company I worked for at the time had a large operation there and needed someone to help the staff deal with the ongoing psychological issues resulting from the earthquake trauma. Having pastored many years before engaging in consulting and leadership development in business corporations, I was selected for this task.

On the flight into Haiti, I asked the Lord to help me. I felt inadequate to deal with this level of trauma even though I had years of good experience. This one could not be handled by past experience or current knowledge. I needed to hear from the Lord.

And then something happened that should not happen to seriously spiritual people in the middle of a prayer session. I fell asleep.

I could not have been out for more than a few moments, but in that short span of time, I had a dream. In the dream the Lord showed me a large ant hill. As I was looking at the hill, someone stepped on it, kicked it, and just generally wreaked havoc with the ant hill. As I watched, the ants scattered, but almost immediately many of them began the process of rebuilding the ant hill. Even before the devastation was over, and surely before a rebuilding plan could be put in place, the ants were back at work on that crushed hill.

> *The Lord was teaching me a lesson that would be used that very day.*

When I asked the Lord what the dream was all about, He said "consider the ant." I quickly opened my Bible to Proverbs to read about the ant. Without a captain, overseer or ruler, the ant knows what to do. When calamity comes, the ant goes to work. I knew immediately that the Lord was teaching me a lesson that would be used that very day. Even though this was several weeks after the earthquake, some of the workers had not yet returned to work. I started looking for those that came back right away. I knew they were like the ant. They would not need a job assignment; they would know what to do simply because it had to be done. They either were, or would become, great leaders in the company.

My next question was, "What is the major issue I will be dealing with, Lord?" His answer was simple: "Fear." And that was confirmed as each person I met, one after another, spoke of fear: fear of another quake, fear of buildings, fear for the children, fear, fear and more fear.

That brought a strange sense of relief to me. Why? Because I knew how to deal with fear. The Bible makes it clear that the antidote for fear is love: "There is no fear in love; but perfect love casts out fear" (I John 4:18). I was able to teach one after another, "the answer to your fear is love. Love for God, love for your family, love for your country and love for your job." You see, when you understand the love of God, and fully embrace it, it will drive the rest of your life.

Since many of these folks were having a hard time returning to work, I dealt with love: when you love your family, you want to provide for them. How do you do it? You go to work and work as unto the Lord on your job. When you love your country, you want to help rebuild it. How do you do it? You go to work and help your company provide the needed services to help your nation become strong. When you love God, you want to obey Him and work hard.

Is it possible to find rest in a situation like this? When the world you have known comes crumbling down around you; when the economy fails, and the housing prices drop, and work is not easy to find; when you can no longer pay the bills; when you are in danger of losing your home, your business, everything materially that you have held dear, is there rest?

The answer can be found by considering what rest is, and what it is not. It is clear from Hebrews 4 that there is a rest. It is also clear that some will enter it, and some will not. So it is possible to either find this place of rest or to miss it.

Rest is defined in these ways:
1. Cease from action
2. Free from worry
3. Be settled
4. Be secure
5. Have something to lean on

The last four items on this list are what we really need. It is possible to be free from worry, to be settled, to be secure, and to have something to lean upon. It is that first one, to cease from action, that confuses us. However, in the context of God's rest, it is not to cease from action, but to be involved in God's action. Doing things for the sake of busyness, or because it is the thing to do, will bog someone down. That is when the pressures start to build and the expected results no longer come to pass. This is also when doubt, fear, discouragement, and ultimately despair begin.

One of the great temptations for God's marketplace ministers is to get so involved in the task, to be so sold out on the work itself, that God is forgotten. The mentality is this: "Thanks Lord for calling me, and I am so grateful to know that work is from you, and I know I can be a minister for you... so now, I'll do it. And by the way Lord, I'll call on you if I need any help along the way." Of course, none of us would be so blatant as to put it that way; nonetheless, the result is we are sold out to God's call but doing it in our own strength. We equate busyness with obedience, a full calendar with full understanding, and hard work with God directed work.

I believe in hard work, and surely the Bible speaks of this as well. Remember that Proverbs passage, the one about the ant? It is there that we are challenged to remember the ant who works hard without being told what to do, and Solomon adds: "A little sleep, a little slumber, a little folding of the hands to sleep - so shall poverty come on you like a prowler, and your need like an armed man." [41] And who can forget Paul's admonition, "If anyone will not work, neither shall he eat." [42] Work is a mandate from God, a commandment that none of us can ignore.

The devil loves to counterfeit the real. Whenever God gives something for our good, the enemy will offer a counterfeit shortcut that seems to fit but that does not. Even with work, if the devil can get us to work hard and to forget God in the midst of it, he will have the upper hand. This happens too often. Work becomes an effort of the flesh instead of a consistent and regular process of staying in touch with the Lord of all. When work is done in the flesh, exhaustion and eventually illness likely follows. When work is done in cooperation with God, a rest comes that brings renewed energy with it.

An easy test to find if you are in the rest of God is to consider how you feel after a long and hard day at work. Are you worn-out, on edge, angry at the world, your family and all those around you? Or are you energized, excited, and can't wait for the next day? When you find yourself on God's path, doing what He calls you to do in His strength, tremendous power is released. That is what I found

Awareness of this reality will revolutionize your attitude toward your Monday – Friday routine.

[41] II Thessalonians 3:10
[42] Proverbs 6:10-11.

with a small group of Haitians. They were at rest in the middle of one of the world's greatest tragedies. They found rest by following a Biblical principle: get involved with what God is doing and find rest.

Several years ago when our family was visiting a large water park, I learned a lesson of God's rest with a water slide. With all of the slides and water activities at the park, the kids were very excited, wanting to do everything at once. My grandson, who was about two years old at the time, wanted to go down the largest waterslide of them all. And he wanted to do it alone. So he and his dad trudged to the top, and even though it looked much higher and more daunting from up there, he started down. The problem was that he was so light, he could not keep his momentum, and just out of sight around one of the turns, he stopped. There he was, sitting in the middle of the water slide, not moving. Of course, his dad was right behind him, coming toward him at full speed. As he rounded that bend in the slide, there was his son was stopped - right in front of him! It was too late to slow down, much less stop, and there was no room to get around him. So, dad did the only thing he could do: he reached out his arms, swept his son into his lap, and carried him full speed to the bottom of the slide.

I liken entering God's rest to waterslide Christianity. We get excited about the heights, the thrill of the ride, the unseen and unexpected turns, only to realize we don't have enough "weight" to carry us all the way. However, when you are on God's path, He is right there to pick you up and to carry you at His speed, with His safety and protection, all the way to the end. God's rest is not ceasing from action, but getting in on the right action. Find out what God is doing. Be involved in His activity, and He will carry you safely to the goal.

104

So let's make sure we understand this Biblical principle. Rest is not 'no more work.' Rest is 'no more work in the flesh.' In Christ the curse is broken, even the curse on work. When Adam and Eve fell into sin in the garden, the result was that a curse came on their work: "Cursed is the ground for your sake." This is where we first identify work with 'toil,' and this where thorns and thistles, and even sweat, enter the scene. [43]

Before the fall in the garden, work was in total cooperation with God. God did the hard work, and man simply found what He was doing and joined in the task. The result was life to the fullest in the Garden of Eden. There were even daily walks with God in the cool of the evening. What a life; what a wonderful existence! And it all came crashing down with the sin of Adam and Eve. For many, it has never returned. That ease of labor is a large part of what Christ came to redeem on the cross. The cross was about salvation for sure, and it is of the highest importance and greatest priority for all. Christ died for our sins and to give us the way, and the only way, to spend eternity with Him.

Another powerful result of Christ's curse-conquering death on the cross was to redeem our work to its original status. I wrote about this in *God@Work II*:

> *God did not plan for labor to be backbreaking, sweat inducing, anxious toil. Instead, He designed it so humans could help Him care for the earth. Meditate on that for a few moments. Almighty God, for whom nothing is impossible, created the world with a plan for men and*

---

[43]Genesis 3:17-19

105

women to help tend His creation. Awareness of this reality will revolutionize your attitude toward your Monday-Friday routine.[44]

When Christ died on the cross, in addition to preparing us for eternity, He was enabling us to be powerfully ready to live life fully today. When we work in our own strength, we soon begin to realize the results of the curse. Some will fight through it by sheer will power. You see them every day: sweating it out, working an extra shift or a few hours more than the next guy, struggling with patience, losing their cool, but fighting to win. The joy has long gone out of the battle, and it is just survival. And some of them seem to be winning, or at least their bank account looks like it, but their family does not.

The "rest" of God allows you to win all the way around. You have peace at night, the family is enjoying you and each other, people are drawn to you, and you still succeed at work. The difference is huge, yet it is accomplished through a very simple principle. Let go.

Did I say simple? It sounds simple, but it is not all that easy. Rest is not easy because we have been programmed differently. We are programmed by society to work 80 hour weeks, to push and shove, to get ahead in any way we can. We have watched others and find that the way to the top seems to be by stepping on, or over, those that get in the way. We pride ourselves in our "work ethic." Unfortunately, often what we call "work ethic" and what God intended as "work ethic" are not the same thing.

---

[44] God@Work II page 26

I know God wants us to work. I am convinced that we were created to work. But our work begins and ends here: let's work with God. Let's find what He is doing, and watch Him pluck us off the slide and onto His lap as we travel the work slide together.

Rich Marshall spent the first several years of his career serving as a Pastor, the last 20 of which he served in San Jose, California, where he pastored a large congregation. During his time in San Jose, Rich led in the establishment of several congregations and saw dozens of missionaries sent around the world in Kingdom work. During these very fruitful years in ministry, the Lord began to reveal to him the very powerful aspect of marketplace ministry.

In 1999, Rich resigned as pastor of his local congregation and began an itinerant ministry to business leaders, revealing to them the call to serve the Lord through their work. He authored two books: God@Work and God@Work II. These books are now published in several languages and are continuing to impact people around the world. He is now working on his third book and the above chapter is an excerpt from this new book.

After a few years of conference ministry, the Lord led Rich to take his knowledge and skills into the corporate setting, especially to deal with ethics issues and people skills in the workplace. Since 2005, he has been working extensively with business leaders in over 50 countries around the world. In 2009, Rich and his wife Wilma relocated to the Caribbean where he served as a leadership and management consultant to several companies. A strong Kingdom minded business owner brought Rich to Barbados to provide leadership with a spiritual emphasis to hundreds of employees. Following a year with these multi-national companies, he spent the next year training with the largest bank in the Caribbean and the largest construction company in the region.

Rich has recently relocated to Colorado where he and his son have opened an insurance agency that provides excellent protection for his clients and a great opportunity for ongoing marketplace ministry. Rich and Wilma are also assisting in the planting of a new congregation in Highlands Ranch, Colorado.

7

TAKING IT TO THE STREETS

by Kathy Tolleson

Years ago I had a vision of a huge army boot coming down from heaven and kicking the doors of churches wide open. People began to spill out, mill together, and worship in the streets. I believe that is exactly what God is doing in this season. Is church still important for instruction, fellowship, accountability, and mobilization? Absolutely, but it can no longer be the main focus of a Christian's life. My husband and I pastored a church in Daytona Beach, Florida for nearly twenty years. During that time, my first language became Christianese rather than English. In 2005, I incorporated a company called ROAR and opened a dealership in 2008. We are a motorcycle company that specializes in products for women. Today my first language is once again English with my second Christianese.

In the first few months of the business I felt like I was coming out of a convent, and in a sense, I was. It took a year for me to adjust to communicating on a regular basis with people who were not Christians. I think that

> *The church can no longer be the main focus.*

is a perfect example of why community impact is so important. It really is the Gospel, the Good News, that we are biblically instructed to spread. Guess what? The majority of people within the four walls of your church on Sunday have heard it. It is your local community that needs the Gospel in living form. That is why the church can no longer be the main focus. In some circles, that statement could be taken as blasphemy. However, biblically, Jesus focused on the Gospel, and the early saints focused on the mandate to go out into all the world and spread the Gospel. The church was easily built as a by-product.

A GREEN LIGHT

Starting ROAR Motorcycles was a huge step for me. Previously, I was spending the majority of my time pastoring, preaching, counseling, and writing. One day I was ministering to someone regarding a generational curse of poverty that was very obvious in their family line. I quoted the scripture, *"You shall remember the Lord your God, for it is he who gives you power to get wealth, that he may confirm his covenant that he swore to your fathers, as it is this day"* (Deuteronomy 8:18 ESV). At that moment, I felt a light tap from the Lord and heard these words: *"I have given you that power, but you have not been exercising it."* I knew it was the truth. In the ministry, we looked more for daily provision and how we could help meet the needs of others but had

112

not been utilizing the gifts and talents we had in the marketplace. That afternoon as I left the counseling center, I repented to the Lord and said that I was willing to use my power to get wealth. When I saw my husband that evening, I told him what had occurred and commented that I had no idea what that was going to mean. Six weeks later, the Lord birthed in my heart the vision for ROAR.

> *"I am a big girl. If the answer is 'no,' I just want to know it."*

I envisioned a company that would specialize in motorcycles, gear, and other related products just for women and felt ROAR was an appropriate name. I love lions and wanted to use a lion for the logo. The Lion of Judah ROARS, lions ROAR, motorcycles ROAR, and we are women, hear our ROAR. It fit. I began to write down the flood of ideas. As with any vision, the big picture is glorious. Everything else is hard work.

My husband and I had been ordained ministers with Christian International since 1991, so I didn't want to take a step of that magnitude without oversight from Dr. Bill Hamon, Founder of Christian International Ministries and our covering. When we first shared the concept with him, he felt we needed to take some time in due diligence and felt the Lord was showing him a yellow light. I incorporated the name ROAR Motorcycles in 2005 and worked on the concept and did due diligence for the next couple of years.

I did not let go of the vision, and in February 2007 at an annual meeting, I once again approached Dr. Bill about ROAR. My exact words were, "Bishop, I am a big girl. If the answer is 'no,' I just want to know it. If it's 'yes,' it is time for me to get going." He prayed and responded, "I see a green light." It was time to get busy.

THE COMPANY THAT FAITH BUILT

I look back now and realize it could only have been faith that continued to move the vision forward. My first test for the Lord was to ask Him to put seed money into my hands. I was clear in my prayer; I asked Him for $50,000, but I did not want the money coming from anyone else. I did not want to raise it, but I wanted it to come through my hands. I knew we would need to raise a great deal more capital for the over-all vision, but it would be a start. I needed a sign, and within a short time, the Lord provided the money. To be honest, I was a little bit shocked.

I hired my first part-time employee, and we started working out of the house. Our desks were two feet from each other but I would call over to her and say, "Hey, Jacki, I just sent you an email." Her first filing cabinet was a red plastic cup which she still has today. At the very first bike event we attended, we had two and a half bikes that we had customized. The "half bike" was the one that looked so bad that we had to hide it behind the tent until we could get an artist to help clean it up. We had no idea how to sell a bike or do the paperwork. When women would sit on our bikes, our prayers were, "Like the bike, like the bike. Please don't try to buy the bike." I had just received my dealership license, and we wouldn't have had any idea on how to process the paperwork. Looking back now, it was pretty pathetic. We wore suede jackets we had bought on barter. They were not even motorcycle jackets but at least they were something. At every step in the process, we used what we had to get to the next level.

Within a short period of time, we found a location for the dealership and had great favor with the landlord, Rusty. He actually financed our build-out, allowed me to design it, and then put it on the back-end of our lease to help us get started. Rusty supplied products to builders, and at the time, neither of us had any idea of the financial crisis that would hit our nation. Florida and our county were particularly hit hard and during these last few years we have continued to support and encourage each other. One particular incident is one we will never forget. In 2009 we had a terrible flood in our area. We had tremendous rains coupled with an intercoastal river surge and bad drainage. The water rose rapidly. Our landlord also had a storage business on the property, so all of the units and their contents were in jeopardy. You could canoe out of our parking lot. As rescue vehicles tried to make their way down the street in front of our building, the wake would cause water to lap at our doors. But I told Rusty, "We are going to pray, and God is going to protect us." The water was about six inches from our doors, but did not enter the building or any of the units. Praise God! Sometimes when you shoot your mouth off in faith, it can be pretty harrowing until the time you see the answer manifested.

> *Periodically, I wondered, "What have I gotten myself into?"*

In the spring of 2008, we opened up the test dealership in Daytona Beach, Florida. It was both an exciting and scary time as we were the first motorcycle dealership for women in the world. Periodically, when I had a moment to catch my breath, I would wonder, "What on earth have I gotten myself into?" Suddenly I was dealing with vendors, employees, and customers from all walks of life. I had never really planned on being the face of ROAR, but in a short time, I realized that whether I liked it or not, I was. It was a whole different world from the one I had become accustomed to over the past fifteen years, even though I had already been involved in community impact.

LIVING IT

Although ministry was our main focus during the previous fifteen years, my husband, Rodney, and I were always looking for ways to impact our community. Early on, the Lord impressed on us that the heart of Daytona was in need of restoration. Like many cities, it was under decay. Drug dealers, prostitutes, and the homeless were rampant. People were avoiding shopping downtown or driving through areas of our community. The first church we established was right in the middle of it all. We had entered a war zone. Everything that was not nailed down was stolen, including sod and plants. We had to have guards outside to protect the vehicles from being robbed while we were in service. There were crack houses on both sides of our building.

Today, it is a thriving church. The crack houses were either torn down or burned down, and you no longer find mattresses in the back parking lot that were used by prostitutes the night before. Another congregation purchased the building from us once we took the land. There have also been two other brand new churches built less than a mile away, and they are breaking ground on a third one. Another church has started in a rental facility only two blocks away. The church is now thriving in that area.

116

In the beginning of the ministry, we worked in the core of Daytona Beach but continued to live in one of the nicer suburbs in our area. It was a beautiful, quiet community. We had a home with a screened in pool. Deer would walk in our back yard. It was a wonderful refuge until that still small voice began to speak to us once again. We felt God was asking us to move to where we were working. It was a big step and sacrifice. We went from a 4,500 square foot home to an 800 square foot apartment in one of the homes we had renovated for our counseling ministry. It was like a bed and breakfast where people could stay while they were receiving ministry next door. So much for privacy.

The next step was the renovation of a 6,500 square foot home that was in very poor condition. Prostitutes hung out on the corners and people cut through the yard day and night. Once again we had to take the land. The house had metal gated doors, so I would laugh and say that we lived in a gated community. I began to use a bull horn to announce to the prostitutes on the corner that this was a "no prostitution zone!" Next, I would say, "Please remove yourself from the area or the police will be called." I put up posters on the electric poles depicting a woman in a seductive pose with a big X over her. The headline read, "No Prostitution Zone." We got a good guard dog to help stop some of the yard traffic. His bark moved people to the other side of the street. Today it's a rare occasion to see a prostitute on our corner or strolling in front of our house. Normally, it's during events when out of town prostitutes come in to work. They do not know about the crazy lady with the bull horn on the corner.

117

Garbage in the yard was also a major problem. There were two convenience stores in the vicinity, and everyone who walked to them would throw paper in our yard. Eventually, with landscaping and constant clean-up, people began to respect the property. We even received a beautification award from the city. Soon other properties in the area were purchased and renovated. We had people in the community telling us that they were willing to invest because they had seen what we had done with the property. The whole area has

> *We would joke about my husband's secret congregation.*

undergone a dramatic change. The house we live in is beautiful now with a landscaped yard. People from all over the world have stayed with us or received ministry within the walls of a home where Jesus took a stand in a neighborhood.

Our second church property was over 30,000 square feet and also needed renovating. It was a haven for the homeless. It was only a block from the downtown area and we had homeless urinating (and worse) in the bushes. They panhandled as people came and went. Again we had to get radical. We had to position men outside the church to help our congregation at service times. We posted a strong sign that said, "We will help you get free, get a job and get right with God, but we will not help you stay addicted, bound, homeless, and lost."

On the other hand, we also did Thanksgiving dinners, backpacks at Christmas, and put a number of them to work. But we had to first earn their respect and take dominion over the property. We have since sold that property to a predominantly black congregation. It was historic because racism is still rampant in our area, and there is still a very distinctive line separating the black community and white community in Daytona Beach. Now for the first time in history, a black congregation has crossed that line. We left our sound equipment, chairs, office furniture, fully equipped kitchen, and a seed offering in every department and area. They were able to have church the first Sunday and walk into a turnkey operation. Their church is thriving also.

While pastoring, we would joke about my husband's secret congregation. Rodney had come out of a business background and had a heart for the business people of our city. He had a whole group of business men and women that he pastored. They rarely or never came to church, but he faithfully brought church to them: stopping in to visit when the Lord put them on his heart, praying with them when they had needs, and speaking the wisdom of the Lord into their businesses and families. So even prior to starting ROAR Motorcycles, we had a heart to impact our community.

CRISIS AND OPPORTUNITY

In 2008, within six months of starting ROAR, our nation and region was in the beginning of a severe economic crisis. By November, I was pretty upset with the Lord. I was having a conversation that went something like this: "Why did you set me up for failure? Why didn't you warn me?" I heard him say, "I did; go listen to the prophecy from Gary Brooks." It was a very specific direction, so immediately I found the tape and began to listen. I remember thinking," I don't remember hearing anything like that. That couldn't have been the Lord speaking." But sure enough, there it was.

119

I remember the day. It was in January of 2008 and the weather was cold for Florida. We had framed out the new dealership and had just started hanging drywall. Gary had stopped in to see us on the way to a meeting. He started to pray and then prophesy. Obviously, I did not have ears to hear at the time yet when I went back to listen, it was very clear. At that time, the housing market had slowed some but we were nowhere near to what happened economically in the fall of 2008. As I listened, I heard these words, "Even in this time of economic turmoil, even when people's backs are against the wall, even so I have called you, and I will write the paychecks, says the Lord." It was there, He had known all along.

I felt a little better, but the natural circumstances surrounding the business were difficult to say the least. I had known from the inception that ROAR would need capital to sustain itself and for future growth but the capital was nearly nonexistent. Credit lines vanished and trying to get people financing for purchases became next to impossible. The one group of investors I had been working with were involved in the oil business and within thirty days, oil prices had plummeted due to a hurricane that hit Galveston where they had holdings, and the banks in Iceland had failed. They had parked the money they had just pulled out of another investment in a bank in Iceland because they were receiving 30% interest. It was gone. That chance of investment capital vanished, and there was nothing on the horizon.

In spite of the challenges I saw people excited about ROAR and knew doors of opportunity were opening. My staff entered me in the Martha Stewart Dreamers into Doers Contest. I remember remarking that I didn't think I was a perfect candidate for a homemaking show. I received a phone call in August that I was one of the top eleven candidates. In the beginning of the phone call I thought one of my staff was trying to play a joke on me. I had just come back from an overseas trip and had caught a cold and sounded terrible. I quickly realized it was the real thing. I was being asked to fly to New York to tape The Martha Stewart Show that November. It was one of the first national media doors to open.

Since then we have received well over a million dollars' worth of free publicity. We were unique and had captured a niche market. The female segment of the motorcycle industry was and still is the fastest growing demographic, yet it is one of the most underserved. I also knew the favor of the Lord was on this business.

Doors were opened, doors that we could not even have gotten close enough to knock on in our own strength. Within months ROAR was featured in Dealer News, a national industry publication for motorcycle and automotive dealers and I was a cover story for Born to Ride. The religious soon began to raise their voices. "You have lost your spiritual mind. How could you be on a cover of a magazine where the Hooter's girl was on the inside cover?" My response was, "If I wasn't there then the Hooter's girl would have been the cover!" We did have to draw the line between certain publications we were willing to be in and those that were just too distasteful to partner with. You cannot be in the motorcycle world without being at events and in publications that reflect the good and the bad of that world. However, we are called to be light where there is darkness, water where everything is dry, and salt where life has lost its flavor.

During Bike Week 2010, CBS Sunday Morning News did a special on women and motorcycling. They came to our dealership to film and then shot one of our Sisterhood Rides. It was an honor to be featured with women like Karen Davidson and Chris Simmons. We also continued to have numerous magazine, newspaper, and online articles written about us. In 2011, Entrepreneur Magazine did an on-line article about the entrepreneurship aspect of ROAR. It was later picked up by MSNBC Main Street. We have also been contacted by several production companies endeavoring to film a reality television show, and we are in serious discussion with one of them. Does the Lord want to open that door also? It would be another huge step of faith but would also give us the ability to impact a national community.

THE WEEK FROM HELL

There were all sorts of battles during the time these great things were happening. The enemy does not let you take new ground easily. Family issues surfaced. Employee issues surfaced. Financially we were constantly in a battle, but one particular struggle stands out. At ROAR we call it *The Week from Hell.* We were scheduled to be in Knoxville, Tennessee for a bike event. We were going to be offering test rides on the WildKaT, a bike we designed in house. We had just made some significant changes in the motorcycle, and it ended up with a belt shudder at a certain speed. Big problem! We decided to take it up anyway for display and work on the problem when we got back home.

I was just getting over being sick. My husband Rodney and assistant Jacki, had now caught the same illness. Part of the team left a day ahead of Rodney and me. Gary, our master builder, had a stroke the morning we were to leave. We did not want to head out of town until we heard he was going to be okay. Finally, we got word that it was a stroke, but he was talking and moving so we decided to head to Tennessee. I was driving, with a sick husband as passenger, hauling a trailer, the WildKaT, and another custom bike.

Because we left so late in the day, we did not pull into our hotel until about 3:30 AM. We were both exhausted and after parking the trailer in a lighted area and backing it up so no one could cut locks, we loaded up the bare minimum and headed to our room. At 7:30 in the morning, Rodney went down to take the trailer and other products we had in our Suburban to the event location. In the meantime, I had received a text from Jacki asking us if we had gotten in yet. I thought it was a bit strange because they should have seen the truck and trailer. Then Rodney called me from the parking lot asking me if the rest of the team could have had a key to the truck and taken it to the event. I said I did not think

I felt the Lord say to pray for our Egyptian.

so and told him about the text from Jacki. You guessed it. Our truck, trailer, and two motorcycles had been stolen from the parking lot! It wasn't just any motorcycle; it was our prototype with hundreds of hours and thousands of dollars' worth of investment. I immediately checked with OnStar and quickly discovered it had been disconnected. After filing the police report, it was time to get something to eat. That is when I realized my little purse must have slipped down between the seats in the truck. I thought Rodney had brought it up to the hotel room, and he thought I had it. My driver's license and all my business and personal credit cards were gone.

While Rodney was filing the police report, I sat in the hotel room basically saying, "What meaneth this Lord?" I felt led to read I Samuel 30. It is the story of when David came back to Ziklag with his army and discovered all of their wives, children, and belongings were gone. In their absence, their camp had been raided by the Amelekites. David inquired of the Lord and received the response, "Pursue, for you shall surely overtake and shall surely rescue." David led his army in pursuit, and on the way, they found an Egyptian slave who had been left behind by the Amelekite army. They helped revive him, and he led them to where the opposing army was camped. David and his men routed the Amelekites and returned to Ziklag in triumph with their families plus the spoils of war. I felt the Lord say to pray for our Egyptian.

The heat was unbearable, the event was a bust, and we also had a potential investor coming in to meet us. I discovered my glasses were stolen also. I knew I was going to have to help drive a vehicle home, so putting first things first; we got Rodney and Jacki to the doctor. They both had bronchitis. I had to find an eye care clinic and buy a new pair of glasses. Our investor came off the plane limping because he had pulled his back out the night before and was also on medication that made him allergic to the heat. We had not one prototype motorcycle to show him and there were no throngs of women drooling over our bikes because there were hardly any people in attendance. The fashion show we were hosting ended up being a pathetic affair because all of our beautiful leathers and merchandise inside the Suburban had been stolen. And it does not end there. We are also Hyosung dealers, and the president of Hyosung motorcycles came to the event because we had arranged for test rides. On his way back to Atlanta, he was in an accident and ended up in the hospital.

I decided to take Rodney home Saturday evening. After we got the investor back on the plane, we headed back to Florida. One of our diesel trucks had a starter go bad at the event, which was a $500 fix, and then when the rest of the team were heading home, they realized the brakes were out on one of our big trailers. It was Sunday and they could not find a place to get the brakes fixed. They had to limp the trailer home through the mountains and the trip took twice as long. The next morning, Joan, our finance manager, discovered she had been robbed while she was gone. Her jewelry and gold were gone. This definitely felt like Ziklag.

We were all shell shocked and exhausted. Monday morning, we began to contact our insurance companies, which was not a simple process because we had private insurance on the Suburban and garage liability insurance on our motorcycles and trailers. We had no idea how they were going to reimburse us for the WildKaT. I started with heading to the DMV to get a new driver's license. That started out badly; the lady at the counter told me I didn't exist in the system. I had a Florida driver's license for over thirty years, so it came as a bit of surprise. The interesting thing was she seemed very content on telling me I did not exist and calling the next number. Needless to say, with all I had just been through, that did not go over very well. I stood my ground, I insisted I did exist, and she finally found me. Somewhere along the line, my social security number had ended up with a wrong digit in it. Something that should have been a simple process had turned into another battle.

125

Jacki asked me if I wanted to cancel the Sisterhood Ride scheduled for the following Saturday. I hesitated for a moment, and then said, "It will probably do me good. I will press in and do it." Saturday morning was there before I knew it - ten days after everything had been stolen. The police had informed us that there was very little chance of anything being returned and that our bikes, trailer, and Suburban were probably already unrecognizable. With every day that passed, we were less likely to have our stuff returned. The lady bikers arrived for our Sisterhood Ride. Some of them had seen our Stolen and Reward pictures on the front page of the website. We had a few ladies running a little bit late, so I ended up sharing the details of the "Week from Hell" as we waited.

Everyone finally arrived and I headed out the door to get on my bike. The phone had rung as I walked out the door. The next thing I knew, Joanie was calling me back into her office. I was a bit irritated because I had everyone waiting. She immediately told me, "There's a man on the phone who knows where our bikes and trailers are." I remember thinking, "My Egyptian." The man on the phone confirmed what Joanie had told me, and I said, "I have offered a $500 reward and if you help me get them back, it's yours." I then had to hand the phone back to Joanie and get on my motorcycle and ride. A lot of details transpired in between but by that afternoon Randy and Kristin Gracy, owners of Southern Biker Magazine and our new found friends from Knoxville, were on their way to buy back my trailer and motorcycles and give the reward to my Egyptian. They had been at the Knoxville event with us, and from the beginning, they had jumped in and helped. The motorcycle community is a close knit group. In a short time after the theft, they had blanketed the area with flyers about the stolen property. Randy had a connection in the police department, and after he and Kristin had gotten our trailer and bikes bike, Randy arranged for everything to be fingerprinted on Sunday so we could pick up everything Monday morning - another miracle. My brother and I, in the vehicle I was purchasing to replace my Suburban, headed to Tennessee.

The Gracy's opened up their home to us and the next morning we went to collect the bikes and trailer. They were covered in finger print dust and the clear glass trailer had some black spray paint on a couple of panels but otherwise everything was untouched. The motorcycles had not even been unstrapped – another miracle. We hosted a lunch to thank Randy and Kristin and some of the women from the Lady Bikers group that had also been helpful during the event and in driving us to doctors and the eye care center. I remember looking at the new vehicle hooked to the trailer and thinking, "It just doesn't look as sharp as my Suburban did. I really miss my truck."

After lunch, we got back in the truck. Earlier I had contacted Jacki about sending pictures to a magazine because they were doing an article about us. I had felt terrible because the day before she had said she was going to rest and stay in her pajamas all day. It was her day off, and I hated asking her, but I knew she was the only one who could find what I needed. I did tell her she could stay in her pajamas, but I really needed the pictures sent out - I could not ask for a more faithful employee. My brother and I had just gotten on the Interstate after I stopped to show him the hotel where we had stayed when everything was stolen when I got a phone call from Jacki. She was very excited and talking rapidly. She said a man had emailed from Texas saying that he had seen our Suburban at a Hampton Inn. He had gone to our website, which was on the truck, and realized it was stolen. She said it is at exit 407. I looked up and saw the exit sign ahead. It was exit 407. We were in the far left lane. I started hitting my brother's arm saying, "Pull over, pull over, I think my Suburban is at this exit." Of course he gave me a look as if to say "you have got to be crazy." But he began changing lanes quickly. As we approached the exit ramp, I saw the Hampton Inn logo on one of the directional signs. I did not see my Suburban anywhere in the front parking lot of the Hampton Inn, but as we drove around back, there was my Suburban – another miracle. The truck was processed through impound, repaired, and made ready for the road. As I drove out of Knoxville in my Suburban, following the trailer and two motorcycles, I had a little taste of what David might have felt like marching back to Ziklag.

We were able to share the story with so many people. Southern Biker Magazine did a whole lay out on it. I had people trying to tell me how lucky I was. I always corrected and said, "No, we were blessed." Someone else said that I had good Karma. I said, "No, I serve a good God." It was a major testimony, even to our insurance agents. It is almost unheard of to have stolen vehicles returned, especially without major damage. The Suburban's dash was pulled out and the ignition broken, but that was an easy fix. Within a short time after "The Week from Hell," Rodney and Jacki were well, Gary was back to work after a short recuperation, and we were back to work on the WildKaT. The investor was impressed at how we handled a tough situation and began to help us with finances for the floor plans. We had acquired new friends and had a great testimony of how God worked in the midst of our situation. The car dealership graciously took the vehicle back even though I had just put 1,200 miles on it. God truly works all things to our good. Hell had not won.

OPPORTUNITIES FOR MINISTRY

There have been countless opportunities for ministry at our business, with customers and vendors sharing heartbreaking stories of illness, death, family issues, and financial problems. We display no obvious signs of faith in our showroom. I had a couple of pictures in my private office that could have given someone a clue, but other than that, it was just the anointing that caused people to open up. I remember a woman, at the first Bike Week we attended, who came in announcing quite loudly that she was ready to buy a bike. The next thing I knew, she had fallen into my arms saying that her husband had just died that week. She wept as I held her. Come to think of it, she never did come back and buy a bike from us, but she found comfort that day.

One day a woman showed up in our showroom who declared to Jacki that she had just learned her husband was dying. She was devastated but heard a voice telling her to come to ROAR and talk to Jacki. She was a nominal Christian and not used to hearing the voice of God. Jacki told her she had come to the right place. My husband was in a back office, so she explained he was a pastor and escorted her back. She was able to pour out the whole story, and then he prayed and ministered to her. It was exciting for us. Obviously, God knew where we were and had a plan.

Without a doubt, we have been able to minister to hundreds of people that would have never darkened the door of a church. That is what marketplace ministry is all about, going into the highways and the byways to reach out to people who are not hanging out at the local church. Let's be honest. An evangelistic crusade is a publicized Christian event. People already have to be searching or sometimes dragged to the event. Crusades have their place, but there are some people who are not searching and will not be dragged anywhere. We also have door-to-door evangelism. Now we are dealing with two issues: first, in the condition of our society, who wants to knock on a stranger's door, and second, who wants to open up their door to a stranger? People can put up a quick defense to hearing the Gospel this way because they have come to expect a certain kind of behavior. Times have changed. Marketplace ministry must be disarming. Few people would expect to get prayed for or prophesied over in a motorcycle dealership or at a tent at a motorcycle event. This is why and how it works.

> *Without the invitation of the Spirit of God, our preaching can be annoying and obnoxious rather than anointed.*

You need people who are sensitive to the Spirit to handle that type of ministry. You do not need the bull in the china shop approach. Some people love to hear themselves talk and will preach to anyone with absolutely no invitation from them or the Spirit of God. They tend to be annoying and obnoxious rather than anointed. If we are going to have Kingdom companies, we need to have Kingdom training for employees. I have been very fortunate because the people in our core team have had a lot of training in ministry. Jacki was a personal ministry assistant for a number of years. Joan has ridden with the Tribe of Judah for years and worked as a bookkeeper for an evangelistic ministry. The Tribe focuses their ministry on outlaw bike clubs. Joan is the national prayer chaplain and ministering in those types of venues takes a great deal of sensitivity. Kati has been raised in church and is a praise and worship leader yet helps with social media and IT. She is trained in the prophetic. Grandma ROAR, Nancy, comes in and volunteers part-time. She is a great intercessor and always knows the right thing to say at the right time. Patty and Ed help bring a spirit of hospitality, prayer, and unconditional love to everyone they come in contact with, whether it is at the dealership or out at local and national events. Sometimes we can show the love of God by just taking the time to listen to someone.

We had one mother/daughter team that came in to ROAR to have a pair of Honda Rebels customized. The mother was obviously undergoing chemo. She was dying but always had a dream to ride. We spent time putting flowers on the bikes and customizing their seats. They were both a bit unreasonable at times, but it was totally understandable. We were able to help make their dream come true of riding together while being compassionate and understanding throughout the process. So many times, unreasonable customers actually have other issues going on in their lives, and if we take the time to listen or just pray, the Lord will give us compassion and understanding for them.

We have a number of women who start riding after their husbands pass away. It is an opportunity to help them gain new confidence and help them through the grieving process. I was doing some personal tutoring with one of these women and in a vacant parking lot we were working in, I confronted her in a loving way on how hard she was on herself. Within moments, the tears came, and she was sharing how hard her mother had been on her all her life. They were estranged. I was able to take the time to minister to her. She rides with confidence now. We have people tell us that when they are having a down day, they just want to stop by the dealership. Why? Because where the presence of God is, there is peace and joy. We live in a world that is hungry for the Kingdom of God, righteousness, peace, and joy; they just do not know it.

THE BIG PICTURE

Our job as Christians in the marketplace is to impact our communities and to be living epistles. Rather than spending all of our time in isolated islands (churches), we have to learn to swim in the waters of the marketplace, government, education, and media. We can all feel like a drop in the bucket at times. The need is so great. There are times at ROAR when we wonder if we are making any difference at all. Then we touch a life, and we know we are.

During the serious flood we had in the spring of 2009, entire neighborhoods were flooded near our business. Rescue vehicles were not getting to all of the people. We mobilized at ROAR. We had our daughter's lifted jeep and another truck that was able to maneuver the flood waters. We went in and rescued children, parents, and grandparents and helped them get to shelters or connect with other family members. We went to the sandbag centers and filled sandbags and then delivered them to other businesses and homes in the area. We delivered water and food to people who were sandbagging and trying to remain in their homes. Our team canoed through neighborhoods checking to see if there were still people who needed help.

In order to impact communities, one of the things we need to learn to do is mobilize quickly to help in disasters and times of need. It is one of the best times to reach out because people are wide open then. We served the community by bringing cleaning

132

supplies and food to a community center to be distributed to people in need. As the flood waters receded, the cleaning supplies were extremely important to deal with the mold and residue. We announced it on our website and had people drop off donations at the dealership. They do not care where the help is coming from and everyone is open to prayer and having their needs met. When we had our larger church building, we became an official shelter. If there was a hurricane, tornado, or other disaster, our church was there to help. We were able to touch a lot of lives during those times.

We have to focus on the big picture. We might only be one business, one organization, or one person, but we have to believe we can make a difference. All of those little drops can eventually fill a bucket. In the spring of 2011, I was invited to speak at an Interbusiness Conference in Curitiba, Brazil. It opened a door to speak at Volvo Manufacturing Company, which has over 4,000 employees. I was able to speak to the innovators of every department. It was definitely one of those moments when I asked myself, "How did I get here?" On the way to Volvo, I was able to prophesy to the gentleman who helped facilitate the invitation. Curitiba is a city of two million people. His family helped found the city in the 1500's. I also discovered another one of the hats he wore was related to the department of tourism.

In July his family visited Central Florida. When he and his wife visited the dealership, I also arranged for one of our representatives from our tourism department to meet with him. There are a large number of Brazilians who visit Orlando and the attractions. Daytona Beach needs more tourists as the economy is hurting. We need to let those Brazilians know what Daytona has to offer so as they plan their vacations they can add our area to their agenda. I can pray for prosperity for our city and I can also facilitate these meetings. ROAR will be an exhibitor in Orlando at a Brazilian business fair. We have invited someone from our Visitor and Tourism Department to attend also. Right now, Brazil is the 7th largest economy in the world and is prospering as the U.S. economy is declining. If the Lord wants to use Brazil to bless our city during an economic hard time we need to be available to help facilitate.

As we "take it to the streets" and allow the Lord to touch every aspect of our society through us, we will face challenges. There will be demonic opposition, jealousy, religious attitudes, and betrayal, but it is such a great adventure. The opposition will take your breath away at times yet the doors of favor will amaze you. The rewards are so great even when the recognition seems to be slim to none. You will build relationships with saints and sinners. Your perspective will broaden. Your heart will expand. Your faith will be tested. Your integrity challenged. Your patience tested. And you will find yourself interacting with the love of God for your community. It is time to take His love to the streets.

Kathy Tolleson is the Founder and CEO of ROAR Motorcycles, Inc. (RoarMotorcycles.com a company that designs motorcycles and accessories exclusively for women. Kathy oversees the ROAR Global Foundation, established to help oppressed women of the world with education, training, and entrepreneurial opportunities.

Kathy is an author, spiritual counselor, and conference speaker who has produced ministry and teaching resources on a variety of topics. Her background in counseling has given her a special anointing for inner healing, and her miraculous salvation and deliverance gives her the faith to see God move supernaturally in the lives of others. Kathy's message to the Church is one of personal victory combined with corporate destiny. People enjoy her ability to bring the truth with love and her most common compliment is that she is REAL.

Kathy and her husband Rodney have been ordained with Christian International for over 20 years. They reside in Daytona Beach, Florida where they pioneered a church and counseling center while fighting for city transformation. Through their ministry, Kingdom Life Now, they have impacted the nations and continue to inspire, motivate, equip, and train both business people and ministers. Together, they have five children and thirteen grandchildren, and enjoy boating, motorcycling, and having time with each other and their family.

8

GOD COMMANDS THE BLESSING

by Mel Ponder

The word of God tells us in Psalm 133 that "when the brethren dwell together in unity…it is there that the Lord commands the blessing." God's intention is for His body to work together in unity: not uniformity, as we are all created with different gifts and callings, but, in unity in the form of working together to achieve God's plans on the earth. The enemy knows this and works hard to keep us apart or cause us to fight amongst ourselves. Unfortunately, the body of Christ has taken his bait all too often.

BACKGROUND

I was born in Ocala, Florida and raised in the Methodist church there. While I cannot remember a time when I did not believe in God or know that Jesus existed and was real, at that time it was only head knowledge. I grew up learning many of the stories from the Bible and understood them to a degree, but it was much later in my life when I realized just how shallow my relationship with God really was.

In college, this shallow relationship with the Lord allowed me to get knee deep in the party scene. I would go from party to party but, in crucial times, was continually drawn back to my Bible. In these times, I would find myself in church every Sunday and sleeping with my Bible under my pillow each

God positioned us to receive an impartation for the marketplace and city government.

night. Even in this shallowness, I knew that there was something significant about God's word and prayer, and I knew that my true destiny and purpose in life were linked to Him.

BROWNSVILLE

The revival at Brownsville, Florida broke out on Father's Day, 1995. My wife Mona and I were members of Brownsville Assembly of God at the time, and we managed her parent's retail stores in Pensacola. We had our first son, Preston, earlier that year in February. Mona and I were working through the changes we were experiencing as parents and in our marriage. So the revival came at a great time in our life.

We attended the revival services regularly, and Evangelist Steve Hill's messages would convict me almost every night, so much so that for a period of over a month, I would go forward to re-dedicate my life to the Lord. I was passionately crying out to have my heart and life right with Him. It was an incredible time in my life as I came to truly understand what it is was to have a heart relationship with the Lord. I was baptized soon after in September, 1995.

CHRISTIAN INTERNATIONAL

Between 1997 and 1998, Mona and I relocated to the Destin, Florida area, and it was here that God began to position us to receive an impartation and anointing for the marketplace and local city government. I had been working for a company called Dean Witter (today known as Morgan Stanley) since 1996, and this created a lateral opportunity to move back to Destin. While walking to the office one day, wondering what God had planned for me, I noticed an artsy fish hanging in the window of a local marina shop. It was then I knew I would promote the "Fish" for His Kingdom purposes.

At this time Mona and I felt the Lord was leading us to purchase my in-laws retail operation. So in 1998, after a time of prayer and fasting, I left Morgan Stanley and Mona and I acting in faith purchased the stores. By this time, we had experienced one of the greatest revivals in our lifetime, I had served in the banking industry, and

"98% of the Body of Christ is called into fulltime ministry."

now God was causing us to become retail business owner's in a predominantly tourist driven economy.

God was also leading Mona and me into what we thought was fulltime ministry. I knew I had a call, but I needed to be pointed in the right direction, and I needed His call affirmed. Keep in mind that this was also when a new movement in the church was being birthed: the role of the marketplace (or workplace) minister.

We were attending Destin United Methodist Church at the time, and I approached the pastor telling him of this unction in my heart to be called into fulltime ministry. He rejoiced and sent me over to the regional offices in Pensacola. It was there I learned that to be in "full time ministry," I needed to go away to seminary for a year, then somewhere else for a year, then back to my home church for a period of time, then I could get into the church side of ministry. We had recently had our second son, and this just did not sound right in my spirit. I did not feel God was directing me to leave my family and pursue this option at that time.

One day, one of our representatives for the retail stores invited us to come out to Christian International to hear a guest speaker. We attended the Friday night service and heard this revelatory message about marketplace ministry. The speaker shared a statistic that will forever resonant in our hearts – "98% of the body of Christ are called into fulltime ministry." Yes, 98% called not just into ministry but into *marketplace* ministry. That was exactly what we needed to hear! Over the next few years, the prophetic ministry received through our relationship with Christian International proved essential in reaffirming to Mona and me our role in His Kingdom.

REVELATION OF DENOMINATIONAL WALLS

With revelation of marketplace ministry, God planted something deep inside of me concerning unity and teamwork in the Body. He birthed in my heart a passion to see His body unified and working in the manner in which He created us to work. So when I observed so many denominations that seemed to separate us, I purposed to be a bridge, building unity in the Body of Christ. I believe that we are so much greater together than apart.

The word tells us in Psalm 133 that "when the brethren dwell together in unity...it is there that the Lord commands the blessing." God's intention is for His body to work together in unity: not uniformity, as we are all created with different gifts and callings, but, in unity in the form of working together to achieve God's plans on the earth. The enemy knows this and works hard to keep us apart or cause us to fight amongst ourselves. Unfortunately, the body of Christ has taken his bait all too often.

RUNNING FOR CITY COUNCIL...AND WINNING

While Mona and I were beginning to see His plan unfold, we had little idea how strategically He was positioning us in our hearts, family, and community to build that bridge. In January 2002, I read in the local paper that only one person had applied for what would have been three open seats for the upcoming City Council election. I was interested. I called a friend that was already running for a vacated Mayor seat. He was thankful for my call and offered to help.

Mona and I somehow knew immediately that our participation in the City Council was God's plan, so we called our intercessor and asked her to pray. It's important to have intercessors to the marketplace minister's family, business, community impact, or anything God assigns a minister to do. Our intercessor prayed and received a word from God that Mona and I were to pray and seek His voice. After prayer, we heard Him say that I was to run for the office of City Council for Destin, Florida.

Time of was of the essence as all of the paperwork had to be completed and submitted by noon that day in a location around 20-30 minutes away. As part of the process we had to open a bank account, appoint a campaign finance lead, and obtain 25 citizen signatures, all within a two and a half hour period.

I walked into the Supervisor of Elections office at 11:59 AM, and the next day's local paper read, "Mel Ponder submitted his paperwork for the City Council election and the race is now on." When I made the decision to run, there were still two vacant seats, and I thought I would just waltz right in and take it. Instead, the election ended up being between four candidates competing to fill three open seats. Yet we knew that the Lord said to run, and we acted in faith even though we were unsure what the outcome would be.

Mona and I walked the streets handing out flyers. I gave four or more campaign speeches to various groups and even stood on a street corner waving to local citizens. We were faithful to do as He told us, which was run, and He was faithful to come through for us. When the votes were counted, I had received more votes than anyone in the election, even that of my friend who was running for Mayor. God showed up big time as Mona and I entered a new realm—government.

The four year term ended up being one of the greatest seasons in my life. God's favor was released to me, and I was able to use my position in the city to meet with local pastors and shed light into the vision and brand for the city. It was during this time that an ordinance for adult entertainment was submitted to the council for a vote, and I was instrumental in working with our land use attorney to make sure all the screws were as tight as possible to prevent it from happening. Thankfully, because of the work done in 2005, future attempts by similar establishments were thwarted, even withstanding pressing legal action.

It was also during this time that the Lord gave me the revelation of the "Blessing of the Marketplace" and what He wanted to do in our community: to build the bridge further, to bless and to unify those who earned their living outside the four walls of the local church, those called to "marketplace ministry."

THE REVELATION

One morning in prayer, I was frustrated and questioning the Lord about our finances and retail operation. I asked Him, "Lord, why is it that since we are faithful with our finances and in covenant with you in our offering, that our stores are not doing well?" In His perfect way of responding, He asked his own question: "Mel, why does the Destin Fishing Fleet do well year after year?" After gathering my thoughts, I responded, "I am not sure Lord, why?" The Lord said "It is because they have a blessing - a pastoral priestly blessing - spoken over them every year." Then He said, "That is the same blessing I want you to take to the marketplace."

He explained that the fishing fleet had done well year after year. They had some ups and downs but overall continued to grow and prosper. The Blessing of the Fleet began with a hand-full of local families who earned their living from the sea. They trusted God and honored Him through prayer, and this blessing in them grew and prospered so much so that today, the Destin Commercial Charter Fishing Fleet is arguably considered the largest in the United States. Amazing! A town with a population of just under

13,000 can boast of having the largest commercial fleet in America. For me, God was equating the principle of His blessing spoken over the fishing fleet to the fruit that He wanted me to see. He re-affirmed to me that it was this same type of "blessing" that He wanted me to carry out into the community as a whole. It wasn't long before God brought the opportunity for me to submit this to the Pastor of the church that oversaw the Blessing of the Fleet, Father Mike Hesse.

FATHER MIKE HESSE

While I was a City Councilman, I felt led to conduct some meetings throughout the town on re-focusing or re-establishing the vision for the city. In my role as Councilman, I was doing a series of meetings called "Let There Be Light." The training was held in four different churches in the Destin area but the focus was marketplace ministry. The invitation was open to anyone interested in attending, and in one of the meetings, Father Mike Hesse, Priest of the Emmanuel Anglican Church, attended. It is interesting to note that Emmanuel Anglican is the founding church, historically, of the Destin Blessing of the Fleet, one of the longest running traditions, not only in Destin but across the entire Northwest Florida area.

At the meeting, I asked him if he had ever thought about expanding the Blessing of the Fleet to cover the other industries in town, such as retail stores, schools, and restaurants "It's funny you mention that," he said. "Just last week Captain Mike Parker approached me about making it more community minded, praying for the Sherriff's Department, Fire Department, etc. I think God's up to something; let's meet!" Over a series of meetings, Father Mike, Captain Mike, and Dave Hope discussed forming a week of blessings to include the marketplace, youth, and other industries in the area, all built around the Blessing of the Fleet model.

THE BLESSING OF THE FLEET AND
DESTIN WEEK OF BLESSINGS

The first year of the Destin Week of Blessing, we held a blessing of the marketplace, which is my passion, as well as a blessing of the youth, a youth concert event, and the traditional Blessing of the Fleet. This event included seven participating area churches, including Christian International Family Church. In year five of the event a citywide picnic was held and we had over 2500 attendees, or over 20% of the total population. This past year, at our 8th annual event, we had an estimated 15 area churches participating in both the Blessing of the Marketplace and the Blessing of the Fleet. The event week has gone through a bit of an ebb and flow, but we have continued to focus on the two main events each year: The Blessing of the Fleet and the Blessing of the Marketplace.

The BP oil spill was stopped miles outside of our harbors.

It is the marketplace event that the area pastors come together to pray over the Mayor and City Council Members, the County Commissioners, State Representatives, State Senator, Superintendent of Schools from two different counties, School Principals from three different schools, Sherriff and the Sherriff's Department, Fire Chief and the Fire Department, Coast Guard, and Military Represented, all in one place, all coming forward, acknowledging that they want the blessing of the priest spoken over them. For me, it gets more moving every year. To watch as a community of business people and city leaders submit as area pastors pray over them and the community they serve is just incredible.

The Blessing of the Fleet is equally important as fishing is one of the biggest industries in the Destin area. When I see the aerial pictures of the boats during the Blessing of the Fleet, I almost weep. Over 110 fishing boats form a big, lazy U in the harbor. As you stand on shore looking at them, you see them positioned in the U, bobbing in the water as they wait for their blessing. They stop working during the event! There is no fishing that takes place—it is one of the most reverent things the Captains do all year. They recognize the importance and power of the priestly blessing being spoken over them and their family, crew, customers, and the seas. It's amazing.

Pastor Tom Hamon, of Vision Church at Christian International, has had the honor of praying protection over our borders the last few years. In the last seven years, Okaloosa and Walton Counties have not had one main storm hit our shores. God has sovereignly blessed us and protected us, and I believe it is because we honor Him through this event and the blessing imparted over the area.

The BP oil spill was stopped miles outside of our harbors. While other areas were hit, we were again sovereignly protected. There is something incredibly anointed about the Body of Christ recognizing that God's blessing is commanded here, and this provides Him with a platform to do something supernatural.

Over the last decade, God has expanded the model for Week of Blessing across the globe. The model itself is extremely simple. Any community in America can apply it. In Destin's case, we targeted the oldest running industry – which is fishing. After you identify a key industry, you call the pastors together to recognize the importance of that industry to the local community. This is the foundation from which to build the model. The marketplace includes the civic officials, retail, tourism, lodging, restaurants, and hospitality—all the key things vital to the community. Next you pray over and pour into them, acknowledging their importance to the success and prosperity in that community. This is not an evangelistic model. The core purpose is to expand an understanding of the power and importance of God's blessings, through the local priest, within city government and in the marketplace.

Through this model, God has opened up opportunity for me to be instrumental in establishing the Week of Blessing as far away as New Zealand and as close to home as Daytona Beach, Florida. After hearing me speak at one of Os Hillman's conferences in Atlanta, a group from Tallahassee, Florida took the model and did a Week of Blessing specifically over the real estate industry for their area.

INDIVIDUAL IMPACT

During the Week of Blessing, we do a corporate prayer over the industries but also have a side room for anyone who has an individual need so that they do not go without having that need met or prayed over. We don't want anyone to leave without having prayer. In these prayer rooms, I love how the local church pastors are led by the Spirit to pray over the people individually. There is something supernatural that happens, and my wife Mona and I hear many testimonies about what God has done.

The prayers are not always specific to business or the marketplace but often address the personal needs of those attending. A hair stylist came to receive prayer over her business, but Pastor Tom Hamon of Vision Church at Christian International, stopped, looked out at her and said, "Ma'am is there something wrong with your wrist?" Surprised, she responded, "Yes, as a matter of fact, I have to go next week for surgery." So he took a moment and prayed specifically for her wrist. Not only did she receive a blessing over her business, but she got healed as well. Her later report was that her wrist was completely healed, and she did not have the surgery. I love how God has His way and does what He needs and wants to do. He just loves to see us come together.

After the real estate collapse devastated the Florida Panhandle, many realtors were struggling. A realtor who attended the Week of Blessings shared, "I understand that people in the real estate market had a tough time last year, but I was not affected." She contributed this to her participation in the Destin Week of Blessings.

A local ministry believing God for supernatural direction for their ministry brought the plans to the Week of Blessings to be prayed over. They could not make it work on their own. When the pastor prayed over them, something broke and shifted. They are now an established ministry focused on restoring broken women and providing them with a fresh start. They shared with us that their ministry was birthed from a prophetic prayer spoken over them at the Week of Blessings

BUILDING THE CHURCH OF THE CITY

God has shared with me that He wants to use me to help His Church transition from growing a church in the city to building the church of the city. Bringing together the Body of Christ, or His Church of the city, is supernatural. With it comes the freedom He has as the Lord to do what He wants to do because His people are getting along. Their work is not about competition or about any particular denomination being better. It's just about what He asked us to do originally. Working together establishes relationships.

Because of working together with churches and community leaders, building relationships, I have greater opportunity in the city. I gained relationship with the schools by serving them, painting their parking lot lines. I now have been able to go to the school principals and get access to campuses for other purposes. Now, looking back, I can see how easy it was for God to open those doors as I obeyed him and served.

Guests who come to speak in our city are all amazed. People from Brazil, Australia, New Zealand, and around the US all say the same thing: They've never seen anything like our model. They say how much easier the ground is here when they come in to deliver a message or a word; whereas when they go into other cities, the ground can be rock hard.

There are a lot of things that you can't describe or plan when you start walking out His destiny in your life. It is years later that we look back and see God's fingerprints. My mother-on-law has a spirit of discernment and has interceded over this area for years. After the third Week of Blessings, she shared the following story with us:

Driving across the bridge leading from Fort Walton into Destin, I felt a spiritual shift over the city. It just seemed different, and I know it is a result of the plowing we have done through the Week of Blessings.

That result is what we are trying to do through the Week of Blessings. We are working to build, expand, and let God have His way in the city.

TODAY'S BLESSING

When the fleet of boats come up to get prayed for, the different participating local pastors rotate praying over them. In each blessing, the boat's name and captain are called out audibly, and then the pastor speaks over them. There is something significant about this. The 2012 Week of Blessings was the largest event yet. Over 380 people were in attendance with area pastors praying over Sheriff Larry Ashley of Okaloosa County and the Sheriff's Department. As they speak, all in attendance observe the moment and acknowledge that in a world of so much separation of church and state, the community is still hungry enough to recognize the importance of this blessing. They lay aside any kind of political agenda or concerns and step forward willingly before the entire community they serve. We invite them to come as guests at our table, at our dinner table. And because they come, we pray blessings upon them.

It is so important for the church to pray for local government officials, and we honor them by doing this.

150

God has given me a great hunger and passion for our cities. My experience in government taught me how strategic it is to have the Mayor, the decision maker, and other policy makers come to the Week of Blessings. Some of these people are even atheists, yet they come to be blessed. Keep in mind that the Week of Blessing is not focused on the salvation message. We are not there to save them that day, but rather to plant a seed so that when hard times come, they will look back and remember the blessing of the Lord. We give every attendee a memorial to take home with them. It is a little desk plaque as a reminder that no matter what is ahead, God spoke a blessing over them. So if it is a government official, we want to release the word into their spirits so that when they leave that place and they are making decisions about adult entertainment, casinos, or anything that could bring potential corruption into a city, they have been girded with prayer and intercession. It is so important for the Church to pray over the local government officials, and it is an honor to them when we do it in this way.

COMMUNITY IMPACT MODELS

While I was Chapter Director for a local marketplace ministry our team would do Business Blessings for local area businesses. Like the "meals on wheels" programs take meals to the needy, the "blessings on wheels" took prophetic prayer warriors into the local businesses. I cannot stress how important it is for a business to have designated intercessors. They are key to the success of any endeavor. While the "blessings on wheels" business owner may be a Christian, their staff may not be, so the spiritual climate over their business can bring great impact. The team would be made up of one or two intercessor as well as those led by the Spirit to minister prophetically over the business.

The Chamber of Commerce does a ribbon cutting for new businesses in the area. After reading an article about it, I realized that it was just as important for the Church to recognize its marketplace people, and Business Blessings was a way to do this. This birthed the idea for a memorial for each business, so we designed plaques that were dated that stated "on this day, this business was blessed." It was wonderful as we prayed for their business, interceded and prophesied, and recorded it all. We would walk through their whole business as they gave us a tour, and then we would take a picture with a banner that read "this business was blessed." We then left them with an audio recording of the prayer and the plaque to stand in remembrance of what God did that day.

In hindsight, Mona and I can see God's hand preparing us for the work we now do with the Week of Blessings. Most recently we established Business Empowered (BE) in Destin. After we initially joined Denis and Coralie Clark from Business Edge International (New Zealand) we branched off on our own establishing Business Empowered. BE is a marketplace ministry established to equip, encourage, and empower business men and women to employ Kingdom principles in the marketplace. We believe that God has called us to BE the church in our vocation.

THE PROPHETIC INFLUENCE

My wife Mona and I have personally experienced the power of the prophetic word in our lives, and because of this, we recognize the importance of it. The five years of training and activation we received while with CI really equipped us to work with the historically denominational culture in Destin. These are fantastic, strong denominational churches that are without a true revelation of the prophetic. Mona and I knew we would have to bring the prophetic intercessory model to the city of Destin and even further west in to Fort Walton Beach. We have a great love for CI, and joined with our heart for the city of Destin, we took this model into the city through the use of prophetic prayer and intercession.

AROUND THE GLOBE

Os Hillman, President of Marketplace Leaders and one of the key leaders of the marketplace ministry movement, has been a guest speaker during the Week of Blessings. We have also had Rich Marshall, Greg and Julie Bailey, and other key leaders of the movement. Os Hillman invited me to be a guest speaker at his annual Atlanta conference. God used that meeting to advance the Week of Blessing model in a Tallahassee, Florida event specific to realtors, and another event in Sebring, Florida where we launched their annual event with a luncheon. Both were birthed from

> *The important thing is that each person understands God has positioned us strategically, so that when He needs to move, we are prepared and ready to do so.*

the Atlanta event. It is exciting to watch God touch someone's heart in these meetings and to watch the model be reproduced across the globe. This reproducing reproducers is definitely an anointing that stems from Dr. Bill Hamon and Christian International Ministries.

Rich Marshall was our speaker in year two, and after observing the model, he said, "Mel, we preach all over the world, and we've never seen anything like this." This was really encouraging, especially after only doing it for a short period of time. Shortly after, he was in New Zealand speaking at a Business Edge Conference, and they were sharing with him that they needed a model for blessing their city. They actually asked him if he had seen any models that would work, and he responded "I've got the guy! Call Mel Ponder!"

This opened the door for Week of Blessings to expand internationally where Mona and I launched the model in New Zealand, with it expanding to Australia, through Greg and Julie Bailey, as CI Australia's first blessing event.

THE POWER OF NETWORKING

Five years ago, God started weighing very heavily on me the homeless in the city. Before He told me these things, I might occasionally see one, but God started to illuminate the men and women around town who were perceived homeless, struggling, or poor and needy. Prior to God's work in my heart on this area, I probably saw them but didn't even notice.

God started connecting me with key individuals who also had a heart to help the poor and needy of Destin. I started reading all the scriptures, and of course the one that gripped my heart the strongest was one in Proverbs: "He who shuts his ear to the cry of the poor will cry himself and not be heard." I thought, "Wow, God, that's pretty black and white." So I hosted a meeting at City Hall, which I was able to do through relationships I had formed in my role as City Councilman.

In just the short week of calling the meeting, attendance included city council representatives, the head of United Way, heads of the local ministries, members of the Sheriff's Department, and a few pastors. All I said was that I wanted to understand what services we were currently providing the city to help those that are less fortunate.

From this meeting, I extrapolated what everyone was doing, and I discovered where I could fit in and make an impact. I truly believe that God uses the relationships and networks that we build throughout our lives. We are using our Business Empowered business ministry and the Week of Blessings models to impact the mountains that God has led us to influence. For Mona and I, it has been a variety of mountains at different times in our lives, but they our woven together, building momentum as we allow God to use us. So far we are in Family, Education, Government, Religion, and Business… and who knows what tomorrow will bring. The important thing is that each person understands God has positioned us strategically, so when He needs to move, we are prepared and ready to do so. And we know He is preparing to move.

 **Mel Ponder** is the President and CEO of Business Empowered, Inc. (BE). BE is a marketplace ministry headquartered in Destin, FL. This ministry equips, encourages, and empowers business men and women to employ Kingdom principles in the marketplace. Monthly meetings, special training, events, and lots of prayer connect this group of like-minded individuals to the higher purpose of bringing His Kingdom into the Marketplace. Mel believes that God has called us to BE the church in our vocation.

Previously, Mel was the Director of Regional Marketing Programs for the Florida Restaurant & Lodging Association. Prior to that, he served as the Executive Director of Coastal Vision 3000/The Beach in Destin, Florida. A Florida native, Mel was born and raised in Ocala. He attended Florida State University and received a B.S. degree in Finance. Mel's past positions include Senior Vice President of the mortgage division for The Bank of Bonifay, Branch Manager for Wells Fargo Home Mortgage, Account Manager with Hershey Foods, and Account Executive for Morgan Stanley/Dean Witter. At Coastal Vision 3000, Mel helped in the creation and establishment of an internationally recognized branded destination for the Northwest Florida Gulf Coast region and served on the team that helped bring Southwest Airlines to Northwest Florida.

From 2002 – 2006, Mel served the City of Destin as a Councilman. During this time, Mel helped establish the Destin Week of Blessings. This annual event unites the pastors and area churches to pray blessings and protection over the fishing fleet, marketplace, families, children, and youth in Destin. Mel and Mona, along with their three children, are actively involved in both their church and community. Mel and Mona have served on the Board of Directors for multiple Ministries, and Mel is the current Board President of Harvest House, a local ministry and thrift store catering to the needs of the poor and needy in the Destin community. Mel also serves on the board of Hope Medical Clinic, established to meet the needs of the medically underserved population in Okaloosa and Walton Counties. He also enjoys serving as a volunteer youth basketball coach. Above all, his primary role is as husband and father.

CI MARKETPLACE RESOURCES

The author contributions in this book are an example of how CI Marketplace Resources networks with other marketplace leaders, together reproducing, reproducers across the globe. Here are just a few of the other products and services available to you through CI Marketplace Resources and our authors.

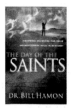 ***Day of the Saints*** by Dr. Bill Hamon, Founder of Christian International, is written with a sense of personal urgency and a surge of anointed passion for God's people. With powerful prophetic insight, dr. Bill Hamon carefully blends the biblical foundations for this event with the spiritual anointing that will propel God's people into the marketplaces of the world. Find this product online at www.christianinternational.com or call 800-388-5308.

Today God is First, offered through Os Hillman and ***Marketplace Leaders*** has a full range of products and services to  equip you to "co-labor with Christ" to see the transformation of your workplace, city, and nation for Him. For more information on the marketplace resources available through Os Hillman, Founder of Marketplace Leaders, go to www.tgifbookstore.com or call 1-888-244-8810.

CI Marketplace Resources offers over 40 different training modules. Instructor Packets include an Instructor Manual,

Student Workbook, and PowerPoint presentation. Also available in Spanish and pdf format in our online bookstore at www.christianinternational.com or call 800-388-5308.

Audio teaching single and full set CDs are available through CI Marketplace Resources. Larry Bizette, Dr. Bill Hamon, Dr. Tim Hamon, Rich Marshall, and more are available online at www.christianinternational.com or by calling 800-388-5308.

 God is showing up in places we have never imagined. He is showing up in small businesses and on construction sites, in schools and in politics. He is in factories and at check-out counters, at nurses' stations and at the stock exchange. God is showing up everywhere outside of where we expect Him to be. Find out more about Rich Marshall, Founder of God is Working and ROi Leadership, at godisworking.com or call 720-536-8454.

Mel and Mona Ponder offer a strong community  impact model through Business Empowered Florida (BE). BE lends support to business owners and leaders, to merge and incorporate both business and spiritual excellence through relational pastoral support. For more information on BE, visit businessedgeflorida.com or call 850-865-0816.

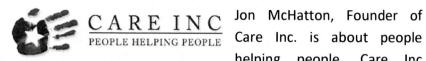 Jon McHatton, Founder of Care Inc. is about people helping people. Care Inc serves the leaders of local government, faith, nonprofit and business communities by providing a safe place for discussion, implementation, action, and service that brings solutions to the needs of people. For more information, visit care-inc.org or call 480.332.9139